Understanding Behavioral BIA$

Understanding Behavioral BIA$

A Guide to Improving Financial Decision-Making

Daniel C. Krawczyk and George H. Baxter

BEP BUSINESS EXPERT PRESS

Understanding Behavioral BIA$: A Guide to Improving Financial Decision-Making

First published in 2020 by
Business Expert Press, LLC
222 East 46th Street, New York, NY 10017
www.businessexpertpress.com

ISBN-13: 978-1-94999-180-2 (paperback)
ISBN-13: 978-1-94999-181-9 (e-book)

Business Expert Press Finance and Financial Management Collection

Collection ISSN: 2331-0049 (print)
Collection ISSN: 2331-0057 (electronic)

Cover and interior design by Exeter Premedia Services Private Ltd., Chennai, India

First edition: 2020

10 9 8 7 6 5 4 3 2 1

Printed in the United States of America.

This book is dedicated to Linda and Sally.

Abstract

People can be remarkably irrational in the complex setting of financial markets and this can lead to catastrophic mistakes costing millions of dollars. We tend to take credit for our successes, but disown our failures. We have limited powers of attention that prevent us from noticing critical factors in investment analysis. Our memories can lead us to make faulty assumptions that serve as the foundation for financial decisions. Our emotions often lead us to give inappropriate weight to some factors while neglectfully discounting others that deserve further investigation. Over the past 50 years, researchers have discovered over one-hundred predictable biases that lead people to make consistent errors.

In this book, we describe the financial biases most relevant to investing, describe cutting-edge evidence of how they develop, and offer practical strategies that can help investors improve their performance by minimizing the negative influence of bias.

We aim to offer readers a book that addresses cognitive bias as it occurs in real financial situations. Not all brain-based biases are the same, but some are more similar than others. We offer the reader a guide to categorizing the different biases based on fundamental brain science. This enables one to implement best practices that guard against whole sets of cognitive biases. We emphasize practical implications of financial decision making and we provide a scientific basis for adjusting practices in investing to avoid common cognitive traps.

Keywords

brain; attention; behavioral finance; cognitive biases; knowledge; memory; psychology

Contents

Acknowledgments..*xi*

Introduction ....*xiii*

Chapter 1   Our Biased Brains..1

Part I **13**

Chapter 2   Attention and the Brain....................................15

Chapter 3   Attention Biases Described 29

Part II... **63**

Chapter 4   Our Memory Systems..65

Chapter 5   Memory Biases 85

Part III **109**

Chapter 6   Knowledge...111

Chapter 7   Knowledge Biases 123

Part IV... **149**

Chapter 8   Best Practices to Avoid Behavioral Bias 151

About the Authors...175

Index 177

Acknowledgments

We appreciate the constructive feedback of several individuals who provided input on this project. We thank Mehmet Gunal, Don Kretz, Michael Lundie, Volker Thoma, Kristine Miranda and John Doukas, for their valuable suggestions and input. We thank Scott Isenberg, and Sheri Dean at Business Expert Press. Special thanks to Russ Stultz for his valuable guidance and wisdom.

Introduction

The idea of a purely rational decision maker has been held up as a gold standard by which to evaluate the quality of our life choices. Economists have discussed models of behavior that represent the rational decision maker. The term *normative model* applies to this case. Economists dating back to the 1800s have called this theoretical normative thinker *homo economicus*, or Economic Man, a person who has perfect information and embodies sound and precise judgment. He is a correct decision maker who always makes the appropriate choice reducing risk and maximizing gain in the most efficient way possible under the circumstances. Economists refer to the normative model when making comparisons to actual human behavior, which is fraught with inconsistencies, distorted estimates, and inaccurate predictions.

Real people act in accordance with what researchers refer to as a *descriptive* model of decision making. A descriptive model attempts to capture how real people decide and includes many of our irrational quirks. For example, descriptive models acknowledge that we have information processing limits, so we will make sub-optimal, or irrational decisions when confronted with the complexities of the real world. The fact that these cognitive errors emerge from our limited abilities to process information makes them at least somewhat predictable and potentially avoidable.

Why are People Irrational Decision Makers?

Over the past 50 years the fields of psychology, economics, marketing, and mathematics have established that people can be highly irrational decision makers. Further, we are irrational in predictable ways. Most investors are subject to some of the same decision irregularities. In other words, if you and I were both presented with the same complex set of information on which to set a value based on the future cash flows of a business, we would likely come to similar conclusions. Furthermore, our conclusions would probably ultimately prove to be incorrect to varying degrees and we may even have made similar errors. The world is too complex and rapidly changing for us to determine the prospects of a business with total certainty. We simply cannot obtain, process, or interpret all of the relevant information that exists. This means that an investor's narrative, or assessment of a company's value, is typically iterative and based on incremental information and future developments. *Homo economicus* is a fiction and we can only aspire to make the most rational decisions possible, but we must humbly remember that subtle biases continually haunt us.

Many market participants and practitioners tend to think of business valuations as static and that they can determine value by thoroughly assessing of the business and its financial history in order to derive the net present value (NPV) of the business's future cash flows. There is wide recognition that the determination of an NPV is only as good as the variables used to calculate it and there can be wild swings in the absolute number based on assumed growth and discount rates. Given the subjectivity in determining the variables of an NPV and the model's sensitivity to variation, the practice of evaluating securities is more akin to Plato's *Allegory of the Cave*, than solving an equation.

In the *Allegory of the Cave*, Plato described several prisoners chained within a cave and situated so that they could only view the wall in front of them (Figure I.1). Behind the prisoners burned a fire allowing shadows to be cast upon the viewing wall. Captors walked along a path behind the prisoners carrying puppets atop poles. A low wall hid the captors, so that only the puppets' shadows were made visible to the prisoners. The prisoners interpreted the meaning of the shadows, speculating about what the "real" objects were. They never really knew exactly what they were seeing, but they could identify patterns debating whether an object was a goat, dog, or a horse. The prisoners' interpretations were all highly subjective, as they lacked access to the objective reality occurring behind them.

Events transpiring within public markets are similar to the moving shadows on the cave wall. Markets differ, however; in that we are placing bets based on our own interpretations and what we believe to be the perceptions of other participants in the future. In this way, we collectively affect other participants' current and future predictions. We

Figure I.1 In the Allegory of the Cave, Plato described a group of prisoners whose perceptions were limited to subjective interpretation of shadows cast upon a wall

Source: Image by four edges CC-BY-SA-4.0, from Wikimedia Commons.

generate narratives to describe a perceived circumstance and price either reinforces or denigrates the short-term efficacy of those narratives. Like the shadows of puppets appearing on the cave wall, securities are symbolic representations of the businesses they represent. Our evaluation of those symbols and our anticipation of how other investors will price them are fluid and dynamic. This is because market participants construct varying narratives and their different analyses can justify a range of possible valuations. Human subjectivity is inherent in markets, so our interpretations are bound to differ at times based on the varying information that different participants possess. You may see a goat, while I see a dog and we may both be wrong (it's really a horse)!

The Relevance of Behavioral Finance

Most professional market participants come from a finance background with proficiency in mathematics or accounting. Investors usually rely heavily on the certainty of mathematics when they apply fundamental analysis of a business's financial performance and condition. Unfortunately, human behavior is complicated, and markets are much messier than mathematical models might suggest. The environment in which markets are made is based on fictional constructs, which are subject to change, interpretation, and from time to time, the madness of crowds. This shifting foundation leads to volatility that is much more drastic than a purely mathematical model would rationally predict.

Behavioral finance is the discipline most directly relevant to interpreting how our subjectivity impacts market events. It is important to factor in the human element when we analyze what occurs in the marketplace, as so much depends upon people's limited perception, memory, and judgment.

Benjamin Graham and the Foundations of Securities Analysis

We believe that the nature of the securities analysis has changed substantially over the last several decades and that those changes make familiarity with behavioral finance more relevant today than it had been in the past. Previously, the volatility of securities could often be discounted because the market was less efficient than it is today. Investors could acquire significant advantages by simply reviewing securities filings that were less accessible than they are in the modern age of the Internet. To appreciate how the practice of securities analysis has changed, it is helpful to understand the perspective of Benjamin Graham, who is commonly recognized as the father of this discipline.

When Graham was writing in the early 20th century, it was common for a profitable publicly traded company's stock to trade at deep discount to the value of its liquid net assets. Graham referred to these opportunities as "net-nets," which are profitable companies that trade significantly below working capital (cash, accounts receivable, and inventories less all obligations payable in one year) less all long-term debt and other obligations. The formula ignored any value that may exist in long term assets such as plants, land, or equipment and focused only on liquid assets. Graham recommended buying these companies at two-thirds of their net-net value and building a diversified collection of them.

Graham described market volatility as a friend to the prudent investor. Typically, an investor is looking to buy an asset at a significant discount to its true or "intrinsic" value. When describing price volatility in his famous book *The Intelligent Investor*, Graham asked the reader to imagine that she is a co-owner of a business with a fictional character called *Mr. Market*, a manic-depressive who periodically offers to buy or sell his share of the business to the reader.[1] When Mr. Market is depressed, he feels that the prospects of the business are undesirable, so he offers to sell his portion of the business at a very low price. At other times, Mr. Market is in a euphoric state and views the circumstances of the business very favorably, so he offers to buy the reader's share of the business at a very high price. Graham advised market participants to ignore Mr. Market's mood swings and to independently conduct a well-reasoned assessment of the value of the business. Then when Mr. Market is being irrational, a rational investor can profit from taking advantage of the spread between the business' true value and the value Mr. Market has ascribed to it. According to Graham, Mr. Market should serve you and not guide you. He should provide you with the opportunity to rationally capitalize on his mercurial mood swings.

The Complexities of Modern Investing

An important assumption underlying Graham's Mr. Market analogy is that the individual investor must be capable of performing a sufficient evaluation of the circumstances surrounding the business to estimate its "true" or "intrinsic" value. When Graham was active from the 1920s to the 1970s, net-nets were abundant. Things are different today. Even if you manage to find net-nets in modern markets, it is more difficult to extract their value. This is because of anti-take-over laws that were passed in order to thwart corporate raiders in the 1980s. These laws currently provide protection for incumbent management and give rise to agency conflicts that could have been remedied with activism in Graham's day. To the extent that these opportunities do arise, they tend to be available among micro-caps and they rarely last long. A massive amount of capital has been deployed to computer-driven quantitative investors that scour SEC

---

1 Graham, B. 1965. *The Intelligent Investor.* Prabhat Prakashan.

US Manufacturing's share of GDP, 1947 to 2017

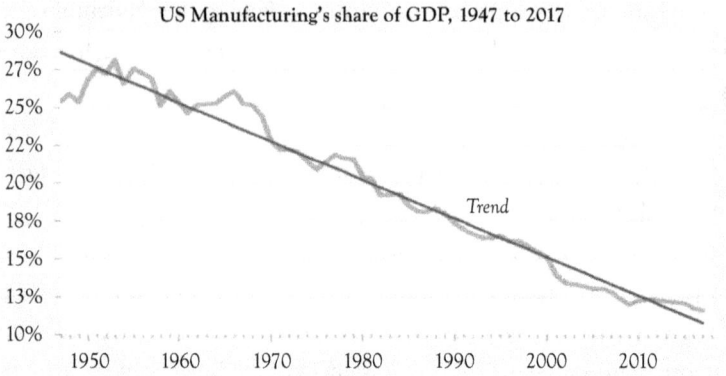

Figure I.2 *The decline of manufacturing as a percentage of GDP in the United States over a 70 year period*

filings for criteria that result in outperforming the market. The net-net strategy is formulaic enough that the algorithmic trading of quantitative investors can close the gap between intrinsic value and market price soon after any potential opportunity becomes available.

Benjamin Graham largely advocated for investing in tautologies where you could literally buy over $1.00 in liquid balance sheet value for $0.66 or less. In an environment where such opportunities were abundant, it was easier to treat Mr. Market as your servant. An investor could act with much greater certainty about the value of the underlying investment premise, which was much more reliable than it is among the vast majority of market opportunities today. It is much easier to identify a tautology like $1.00 is worth more than $0.66, than it is to predict a business's future prospects.

Today, most securities analysis depends upon predictions about the direction of future cash flows. When Graham was evaluating net-nets, he had a high level of certainty about the company's value at the time of the investment and he did not have to devote much, if any, consideration the future of the businesses he was looking to invest in. The economy was also significantly different in the early 20th century than it is today. In that earlier era, manufacturing was more than two-and-a-half times larger as a percentage of the economy (Figure I.2). Most companies had significant tangible assets. Today, the economy is much more oriented toward services and intellectual property. Asset values typically represent significantly less of a company's value. When modern investors evaluate

The uncertainty continuum

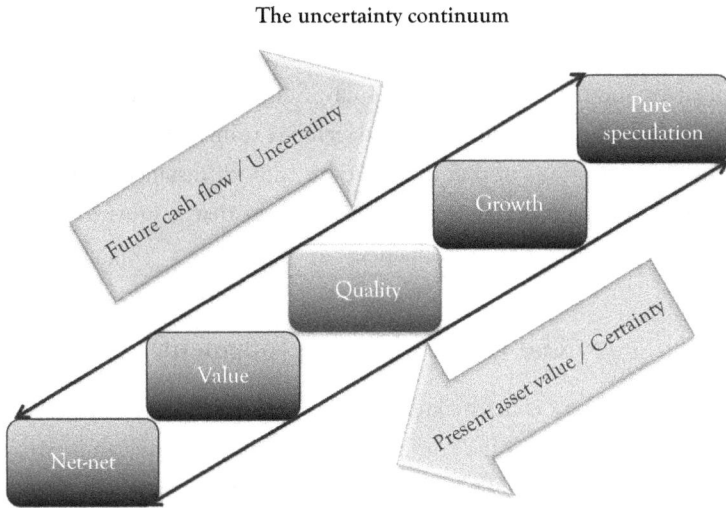

Figure I.3 The uncertainty continuum describes a variety of investment opportunities in terms of their levels of risk and opportunity

financial statements, they place greater emphasis on the income statement, revenues, and profits than the balance sheet.

There is a continuum of uncertainty among different types of equity investments (Figure I.3). The most certain investments at the lowest end of the uncertainty continuum are net-nets where the liquid assets of the business are easily discernable from the company's balance sheet. As we move up the continuum there is ever-greater reliance on projections of the future as the basis for a rational investment. With each step upward, the investor can rely less on the current state of affairs and must increasingly rely upon less certain future developments.

The more our analysis relies upon determining events in the future, the more likely it is that we must rely on a prediction narrative. We must monitor data points as they develop and then extrapolate them into trends. Reliance on a predictive narrative creates uncertainty, which is where bias is much more difficult to overcome. The higher we move up the uncertainty continuum, the observable data become darker and murkier. Under these circumstances, the process of security analysis turns into a sort of psychological Rorschach test that often better reflects the investor's mental state than the company he is trying to analyze.

Today, the questions raised when evaluating investment opportunities involve a much greater degree of subjectivity than what was required for evaluating the net-nets of Graham's day. Subjectivity is present in both information that is provided by management teams and market participants' interpretations of that information. In both instances, psychological bias may creep in coloring the information that is provided and its interpretation by market participants.

The Role of Human Judgment

Investment success is hardly guaranteed, as we are limited to processing only a select amount of the relevant information. Thus, we can be wrong about "intrinsic value," we can be wrong about how others will estimate value, and we can be wrong about why a security is priced the way it is currently. We cannot know, perceive, or interpret everything possible. The natural limitations of our thinking force us to attend to some subset of the possible information relevant to value at any given point. Consistently great investing requires us to prioritize certain information, keeping in mind that our analysis is based on incomplete information, likely has flaws, and is subject to change. There is no guarantee that any single investment will be successful regardless of the superiority of our analysis. Nonetheless, if you can implement sound processes for data collection and conducting your analysis, then over time and multiple investment opportunities you can tilt the odds in our favor and enjoy sustained success.

Our Approach to Addressing the Challenge of Behavioral Bias

Our principle focus is to classify, describe, and help you to remedy errors that are made during fundamental analysis. Typically, errors occur during data collection and the implementation of the investment processes. You can have an impact on your performance if you utilize disciplined practices to avoid errors during these critical points in time.

Over the last 20 years, there has been increasing interest in behavioral finance and the role of bias in investment decisions. This discipline provides insight into how behavioral biases and cognitive errors influence individuals' investment decisions. Several books have been written on the subject and it has been incorporated in the Chartered Financial Analyst course of study. In this book, we offer you a new perspective that emerged from our joint expertise. We present a framework to help you understand behavioral biases, along with a wide-array of practices that you can implement in order to mitigate their harmful effects.

Some behavioral investment bias books are written by academics with limited experience participating in the public markets, while others are authored by investment advisors with a limited knowledge of the science behind this topic. Much of the current literature describes a litany of behavioral biases, which often bleed into one another without clear distinctions regarding their nature, or their origin. Linked to this fuzziness, the existing literature offers limited guidance on how to remedy the deleterious effects of our biases.

The state-of-the-art in behavioral bias often reduces to two things: (1) describe the existence of heuristics and cognitive biases and (2) cast dire warnings that these are extremely difficult to avoid. This often leads readers of the judgment and decision-making literature to think of biases as being unfortunate and perhaps unavoidable consequences of our cognitive architecture. Investors remain in the challenging position of questioning their own judgment and possibly being less confident in their analyses, while lacking guidance on which biases might be influencing them and how to counter them.

This book represents a fusion between the academic perspective and market experience through the collaboration of an academic cognitive neuroscientist and a practicing hedge fund manager. While biases are indeed challenging and unsettling, we aim to help investors to better understand how various biases are interrelated. We refer the reader to real-world examples based on actual investment situations to illustrate how cognitive biases distort our investment decisions. We offer a categorization of behavioral biases based on their emergence from common cognitive and brain functions. Brain-based mechanisms that deal with information processing limits lead us to take certain types of mental shortcuts in the form of biases.

Armed with an understanding of how different types of biases occur, you will be in a better position to minimize their potentially toxic influences on your investing practices and perhaps to identify potential distortions haunting the minds of others that might create the opportunity for profit. To assist you in addressing the bias in your research and analysis we provide a full chapter of suggested best practices to defend against your own biases and capitalize on the bias-induced mistakes of others.

We have included a diversity of quotes throughout the book. These emphasize the *feel* of grappling with bias and add color to the narrative. They were selected from a wide range of individuals from science, finance, politics, fiction, and history emphasizing the universal nature of biases.

> *To give a satisfactory decision as to the truth it is necessary to be rather an arbitrator than a party to the dispute.*
>
> —Aristotle

CHAPTER 1

Our Biased Brains

Heuristics and Biases

A *heuristic* is often defined as a "rule of thumb," or mental shortcut. A stop-loss rule is an example of an investing heuristic. Investors can limit their losses at a given price point mitigating the risk that any individual issue may pose to their portfolio. Many investors can recognize when they are on the unfortunate side of a probabilistic determination, or when they face a more significant risk than planned when the price does not reflect their narrative. They then rely on the stop-loss heuristic to overcome the possibility of an undesirable result or analytical misjudgment based on their past experience in similar circumstances.

Biases are tendencies to process some information differently based on the current circumstances. A bias toward certain thoughts or behaviors can emerge for a variety of reasons. Heuristics and biases are related. Heuristics derive from biases that we develop. Most biases emerge over time and they are shaped by our experiences. Biases lead us to act a certain way under certain conditions. Our biases are linked to what we have experienced and our expertise level. An expert in technology investments will hold a variety of biases that are driven by a set of situations that they have seen play out time and again in that industry. As such, the expert can often act with an intuitive sense. By contrast, the novice will need to devote much more time and resources to evaluate appropriate value.

Let's consider a now famous example, Daniel Kahneman and Amos Tversky's *representativeness heuristic*. Coin flips provide an illustrative example of this bias in action. A sequence of seven heads in a row feels contrived and improbable, while a sequence containing a healthy mix of heads and tails feels more probable. The mixed sequence looks random, as most do, while straight heads seems like a rare circumstance. The coin flip example captures a heuristic that leads people to prioritize their own intuitive feelings over statistics. We know that the probability of a head or tail flip is always 50 percent regardless of the previous number of sequential outcomes, but the run of heads feels different to people. This example illustrates that we judge sequences or situations to be more probable if they look like "good representatives" of the distribution from which they are drawn.

Biases and heuristics can sometimes help us. The expert gets through his day making relatively confident decisions using fast intuitive judgments. Experts become trusted analysts and advisors because they are correct a lot of the time and their bias-driven heuristics come to be appreciated as tools to be rapidly deployed, while less experienced decision makers scramble to understand the basis for unexpected changes.

There is an ominous dark side to heuristics and biases as well. The expert who is driven by biases may be wrong in an important analysis due to careless over-application of his heuristics. We often act on our biases in an intuitive fashion. They feel right. We do not question them. This expediency can lead to errors when more analysis is called for. A heuristic can emerge and steer us astray during a key decision because the surface characteristics of a situation appear to match a well-developed and previously successful tendency. We are wrong some of the time when we follow our biases because we have misread the surface situation. What's worse, we usually walk right into our own trap when our simplified version of reality differs from what is actually going on.

Biases Emerge from the Limited Information Processing Power of Our Brains

Biases are based on how we make sense of the world using our limited powers of attention, memory, and knowledge. Biases lead us astray when solving thought problems. This is particularly troublesome when we make quantitative estimates. We rely on biases when information is abundant and complex. We also rely on biases when a situation reminds us of something we have seen many times before. In other words, precisely the type of information processing that must be accomplished in investment analysis can lead us to make inappropriate thinking errors based on our biases.

Mental Blind Spots: The Brain's Behavioral Biases

A key point for investing is that the brain builds an *incomplete* internal mental model of the outside environment. This incomplete model is also distorted by the particular details to which we attend and those that we miss. When you build a narrative on a company, it will be somewhat distorted, as you can only attend to a subset of the information available. Further, many investors tend to exaggerate the importance of the attended information to the exclusion of the things they missed. Those missing details can turn out to be critical.

The brain is like the proverbial blind men who attempt to describe an elephant as they each examine different parts of the animal by touch (Figure 1.1). Like the different men experiencing sensory differences between the tusks and the skin, our sensory systems take in different parts

Figure 1.1 The proverb of the blind men and an elephant. Each man can describe only part of the elephant based on his limited experience

Source: Public domain image from Wikimedia Commons.

of the environment. Just like the blind men, the brain misses key aspects of the incoming information and this leaves us with gaps in our understanding. Unlike those arguing men who struggle to agree on the true nature of the animal, our brains generate a mental model of the narrative that *feels* very real to us. We can think of this as a somewhat incomplete mental sketch of reality. Through filtering and integrating the information, the brain resolves inner conflict and our conscious minds feel as if our narratives are closer to reality than they really are. This is a key part of why cognitive biases persist *even after we become aware of their presence.*

Knowing about biases may be "half the battle," but that's not quite enough to conquer their undue influence. We will also discuss methods that will help you to overcome many of these attention biases through your work, or at least minimize their undue influence on your portfolio outcomes. We will next provide you with some introductory information about the brain that is relevant to understanding how it generates behavioral biases.

> *and knowing is half the battle*
> —Roadblock, (G.I. Joe Public Service
> Announcement)

The Brain: An Overview

Your brain weighs approximately three pounds with much of this mass being made up by its outer layer, the cortex. The cortex is too large to fit around the small surface of the brain, so it is folded into a series of bumps and valleys. Species with small amounts of cortex have smooth brains, while organisms with large amounts of cortex have highly convoluted brains. Small, smooth brains have less processing power and typically generate simpler behavior. Species with large cortical mass include dolphins, elephants, and great apes. Like us, these species lead complex social lives and engage in a sophisticated array of behaviors. They likely possess some degree of consciousness as well. Our cortex has allowed us to develop monetary systems and the ability to mentally simulate the future to make predictions about value.

Neurons: the brain's processing power: Our huge cortex contains billions of electrically active cells called *neurons* (refer to Figure 1.2). Neurons communicate through an electrochemical process called the *action potential*. Neurophysiologists commonly refer to action potentials as *spikes*, in which the neuron moves from a negative polarity state to a positive one and back again in just a fraction of a second. The spikes form the ones and zeros in the brain's binary code, similar to computer software. Also, like computers, our brains are networked by insulated high-speed connections called *axons* (Figure 1.2). Bundles of axons form large-scale *tracts* and these tracts comprise the information superhighways of our brain. Our brains operate by delivering and receiving electrically coded messages, sometimes across long distances within the brain.

Two types of tissue are most obvious when looking at the brain. The *grey matter* is made up of binary code generating cell bodies, while the bundled tracts form the *white matter*. The presence of tracts gives us a strong clue about brain organization. Some regions are wired up to communicate directly, while other areas route their signals indirectly through relay points involving several neurons. We often act on the messages that arrive first, so both cortical distance and spike timing are key factors linking brain processing to action. This is similar to how we act in our daily lives, as we communicate more with those closest to us and those already entered into our contacts list. This is a key feature of the brain that helps to explain our biases: we are quicker to act on some information and slower to make use of other details depending on the speed of our brain's associations.

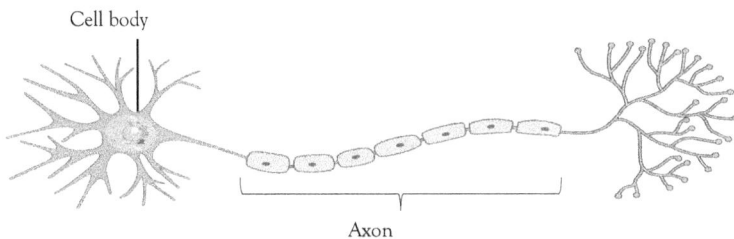

Figure 1.2 The structure of a neuron. An electrical action potential is generated within the cell body and transmitted down the axon influencing other connected neurons

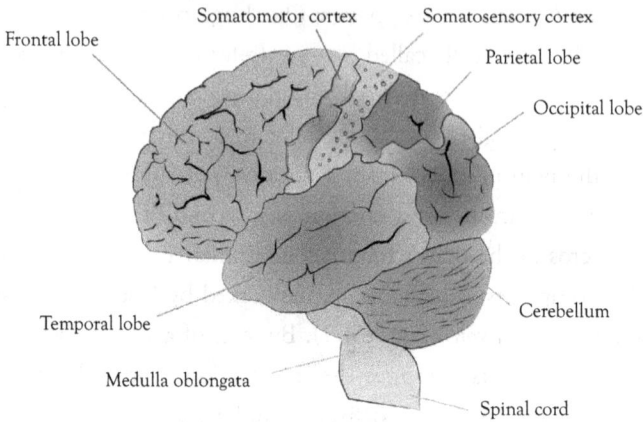

Figure 1.3 The brain is divided into several regions. The frontal lobes, temporal lobes, parietal lobes, and occipital lobes represent major divisions

Source: Image by Jkwchui CC-BY-SA 4.0, from Wikimedia Commons

Lobes and hemispheres: Just as continents divide into countries, your brain divides into several anatomically distinct areas called *lobes*. The lobes offer another clue about brain organization (Figure 1.3). People used to refer to math as being a *left brain* function, while artistic creativity was thought of as a *right brain* ability. This is far too broad a generalization for most modern scientists. It is more useful to divide the lobes according to *anterior* and *posterior* functions, as these relate to how our minds process and act on information related to value.

Joaquin Fuster, an esteemed neurophysiologist, spent many years carefully examining the brain's neurons and how they enable memory and incentive-driven behavior. Krawczyk first heard Fuster speak when he was in graduate school and has watched his insightful talks many times over the years. Fuster was the first scientist to report frontal lobe neuron spiking related to memory in 1971.[1] Despite his focus on recording the activity of single neurons, Fuster provides a visionary sense of the brain's connectivity. He refers to the brain carrying out a *perception-action cycle.*[2]

---

[1] Fuster, J.M., and E.A. Garrett. 1971. "Neuron Activity Related to Short-Term Memory." *Science* 173, no. 3997, pp. 652–654.

[2] Fuster, J. 2015. *The Prefrontal Cortex.* Academic Press.

Fuster points out that the back of the brain largely specializes in *perception,* or information *intake*, while the frontal lobes specialize in *action*, or behavioral *output*. Perception and action are linked by the brain's vast white matter connections. Both operations are important for understanding and alleviating behavioral biases.

Decades of research and thousands of studies confirm that there is a clear division between perception and action, which is mirrored by the brain's anatomy. Our brains take in sensory inputs and build them into a *mental model*, or sketch of the environment. The mental model is like a coded image based on the limited set of available information that we can attend to. The front of the brain filters that mental model and then initiates action based on that filtered reflection of reality. This is a key point explaining our behavioral biases—we operate based on a subjective model of reality.

> *The eye sees only what the mind is prepared to comprehend.*
> —Robertson Davies

Distortions of value can occur based on fear and greed. The brain circuits that we use to explore our environment for rewards and to exploit those opportunities lead us toward these distortions. They occur commonly across many people, since we all invoke similar brain activity when we are driven to obtain incentives and avoid losses. By gaining a better understanding of our brain circuitry related to incentives, we can begin to predict when we will be vulnerable to bias. By understanding groupings of biases related to our attention systems, we can develop processes, and systems that will help us to avoid these traps.

Categorizing Biases

We present behavioral biases in three different categories. These groupings are largely based on common cognitive processes and associated brain functions that give rise to the bias. We begin with Attention Biases, followed by Memory Biases, and conclude with Knowledge Biases.

While these groupings are not absolute, categorizing the biases helps us to make sense of their origins and allows us to apply common remedies across interrelated biases. We make note of particular biases that relate to one another most directly in the subsequent chapters.

Attention Biases

Attention biases emerge from the way that our brains process incentives. Particular regions of our brains have been tuned over years of evolution to enable foraging behavior. Essentially, we are all walking around with genetic predispositions hard wired in our brain circuitry that are suited for survival as hunter-gatherers over 40,000 years ago. You can think of these brain areas as survival circuits that help us learn what conditions lead to rewards and how to change our behavior in the face of losses. Money is such a potent incentive in our daily lives, that we engage these same circuits when we make monetary decisions.

We will address attention biases in Chapters 2 and 3 and offer suggestions to address these biases in Chapter 8. Many of these biases involve attending to some information too selectively when it has been connected with prior gains, while we perilously ignore key information because it is inconsistent with our belief in a particular thesis. Ultimately, troubling cognitive illusions can develop from our attention systems and these must be actively avoided.

Memory Biases

Human memory is flawed. There is simply too much incoming information to remember all of it, so our brains take shortcuts by selectively remembering certain information and forgetting the rest. This leads to biases that negatively impact investing.

Let's try a brief thought experiment. What did you have for lunch yesterday? The day before? Over the past weekend? Exactly two weeks ago? Exactly one month ago? This date last year?

If you were able to answer even half of these accurately, you did very well. You likely could produce yesterday's lunch items quickly and almost effortlessly. As you moved back in time, it became more difficult to imagine the circumstances and details to recall a specific lunch order. Going back even two weeks is quite difficult and beyond one month almost impossible. There are hard limits on the information processing capacity of our brains. Our faulty memory systems provide a clear example of this challenge. Your brain processes recent events quite differently than older events. We generally lose detail over time and even distort memories to fit our current viewpoint. Our brains gloss over some of the details rather than store all of our experiences in as much detail as possible. We retain some core features of an experience, while losing many of the peripheral aspects of the situation.

Like attention biases, we can group biases that emerge from our memory systems. Some of these biases include inappropriately prioritizing certain information from our personal memories. These can distort our narratives over time because our memory systems accommodate new information in an unbalanced fashion. Once we review this category of memory biases covered in Chapters 4 and 5, we offer steps to address these biases in Chapter 8.

Knowledge Biases

Knowledge biases stem from the interactions between new incoming information and what we have experienced repeatedly in the past. The brain is highly attuned to suggestion. We actively fit new information to structured sets of older information as we construct and evaluate investment narratives. These knowledge structures are built up over time as we notice repeated trends, tendencies, and similarities among narratives. Researchers call these structured knowledge sets *schemas*. Schemas form the basis of our general knowledge about the world. They are plastic, in that we modify them through our experiences. Sometimes our active information processing leads to an altered schema as we observe a trend repeatedly. Alternatively, schemas can work in reverse by altering our information processing so that it fits with what we already know. This leads to a set of biases that can be destructive to investing.

Understanding the nature of knowledge biases can lead to more objectivity, better narrative construction, and an enhanced ability to appropriately weight incoming information. Taking active steps to keep a level head and calibrate your assessment of incoming information will help you to be right more often, spot more opportunities, and more effectively take advantage of them. We cover knowledge biases in Chapters 6 and 7 and we offer steps to address these biases in Chapter 8.

Organization

This book is divided into four brief sections:

- Section I (Chapters 2 and 3) covers biases that emerge from our attention systems. Chapter 2 will provide you with some key background information on attention and the brain, while Chapter 3 will describe the cognitive biases related to the functions of our brain's attention systems.
- Section II (Chapters 4 and 5) focuses on memory biases. In Chapter 4 you will learn about the functioning of our brains' memory systems and how these introduce distortions and biases that can affect investing behavior. Chapter 5 describes a category of biases related to memory.
- Section III (Chapter 6 and 7) presents knowledge biases. Chapter 6 focuses on the nature of knowledge and the brain systems that underlie this critical human ability, while Chapter 7 presents biases that emerge from what we know about the world. By presenting you with three interrelated sets of biases, we hope that you will better understand their origins, which may help you to effectively mitigate whole sets of cognitive biases using a limited set of targeted techniques.
- Section IV (Chapter 8). This last chapter provides guidance offering best practices and advice geared toward minimizing the undue influence of heuristics and biases in your investing process. We believe that employing these techniques will enable you to remain vigilant and objective without having to take on each and every individual bias one-by-one.

We may not be able to completely eliminate investing mistakes that stem from biases, but we can take concrete steps to minimize the possibility of cognitive errors by consistently deploying methods that help us to be more objective. Rather than trying to fight dozens of small fires created by the many biases that have been identified over the years (the Wikipedia list of cognitive biases named over one hundred biases at the time of this writing), investors can address whole sets of inter-related biases using specific best practices detailed in Chapter 8.

For ease of use, you can read brief descriptions of the remedies and best practices at the end of each description of each individual bias (in Chapters 3, 5, and 7). This will help you to easily locate our recommendations for addressing individual biases. Using the book in this way may help you to address specific biases that you are particularly concerned about, or ones you have noticed in your colleagues. The ability to read about individual biases may also prove handy as you reflect on times when bias may have undermined your performance, or when you find yourself in situations that make you vulnerable to investing-related heuristics or biases.

Objective analysis is difficult. We have a particularly challenging time understanding our own biases, as consciousness is an engine of subjectivity. Minimizing bias requires self-study and outside analysis. It also requires keeping an open mind and incorporating new elements into your investment process. Easy access to advice on specific biases will help you to become your own best advocate for avoiding subjectivity and becoming a stronger performer.

It is an acknowledged fact that we perceive errors in the work of others more readily than in our own.

—Leonardo da Vinci

PART I

CHAPTER 2

Attention and the Brain

Attention Processes

Intuitive and Analytical Thinking

Many researchers have proposed that we engage in two modes of thinking: a fast, automatic, and *intuitive* mode, along with a slow, controlled, *deliberative* mode.[1] We often refer to the intuitive style as thinking with your "gut," while we call the analytical mode thinking with your "head." People are referring to these two modes when they advise you to "trust your gut instinct" and "just do what feels right," or when you hear someone say "think it through" and "don't rush to judgment." The "gut" is intuitive and filled with emotion. It is usually considered to be inferior to the "head," suggesting that intuitive judgments are ill-informed and hurried, while analytical judgments are always carefully constructed and well-developed.

In reality, we use *fast/intuitive* thinking effectively for some judgments and *slow/analytical* thinking for others. The quality of our thinking style is not quite so easily determined. For instance, the intuition of an expert is often superior to the careful analysis of a novice. Behavioral biases frequently arise from our distorted intuition, but some biases emerge when we devote too much thought to a problem. The amount of attention that we allocate to a problem is strongly related to what we casually consider the modes of thinking.

While thinking style is an academic topic that can feel somewhat detached from reality, focusing our attention on different inputs *feels*

---

[1] Evans, J.S.B. 2003. "In Two Minds: Dual-Process Accounts of Reasoning." *Trends in Cognitive Sciences* 7, no. 10, pp. 454–459.

quite real to us. When we devote our attention to a problem, we struggle with the mental effort to think hard and deliberately. By contrast, when we are in a low attention, *intuition* mode, we feel fast, loose, and capable of performing other demanding tasks while we decide.

Our modes of thinking are strongly linked to brain physiology. Krawczyk's career has often straddled the line between brain science and human behavior. We need to understand both to mitigate biases effectively. We next focus on whether these two modes of thought are actually present at the level of the brain. We think there is evidence for both modes, but the answer is a bit more complex than a simple division between thinking with more or with less attention.

Thinking with Our Brains

There are rarely just two modes in an organ as complex as the brain. The brain must rapidly navigate us through a burning forest, just as it navigates us through the countryside on a peaceful stroll. Several features of a situation determine which parts of the brain become active to solve a particular problem. These include emotional context, the necessary speed of response, and the type of action required. More accurately, these factors determine which brain *networks* respond, as neurons act in large numbers communicating *en masse*. Two critical factors determine which brain networks respond in a given situation: *response time* and *information complexity*.

Figure 2.1 presents an inverted pyramid representing three major types of brain network responses that drive our investment thinking. This pyramid was developed by Krawczyk and his colleague, Adam Teed. At the bottom is the narrowest set of responses (lowest information complexity) that we deploy fast and automatically. We refer to this as the *instinct* level. Above instinct is the level of *intuition,* a wider array of possible behaviors that also occur relatively automatically, but more slowly. At the top of the hierarchy is the *reason* level: those mental abilities most accessible to consciousness and most developed in our large cortex. Processing at the reason level involves the highest information complexity and takes the longest. We will next consider each of the levels individually as they relate to investing and behavioral biases.

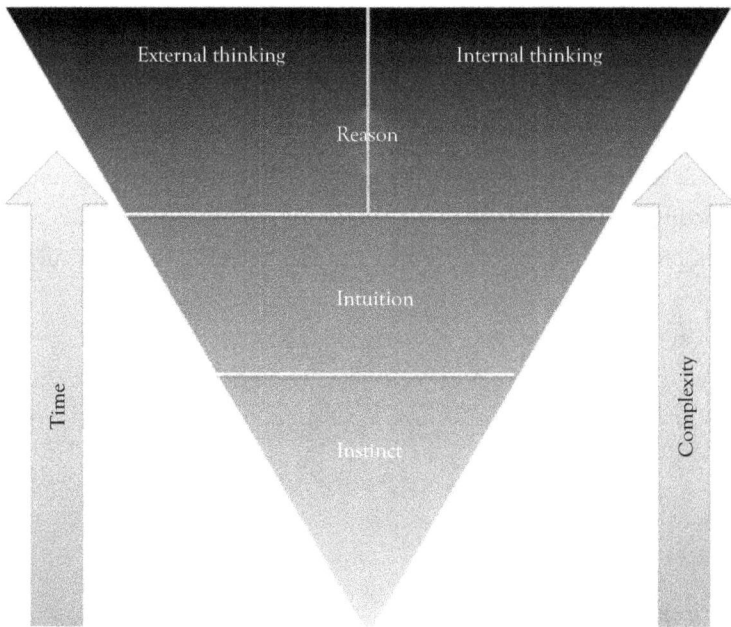

Figure 2.1 Instinct, intuition, and reason divide based on speed and information complexity with the narrowest responses at the bottom and the widest array of responses at the top. Reason further subdivides into our external and internal thinking.

Instinct

Instinct is our first and fastest mode of thinking. It supports our "fight or flight" survival responses. At a baseball game, we duck almost reflexively when a foul ball is hit hard toward our heads. We run in fear when an angry pit bull charges at us. We become keyed up and ready to run when we see expressions of fear in the people around us. These instinctual responses require almost no effortful thinking. They are highly automatic and are expressed very similarly across different people. We have little control over these feelings; they simply emerge. Instincts also guide us when we are confronted with threats or highly potent rewards.

When people discuss fear and greed in investing, the amygdala emerges as a frequent topic of conversation. The amygdala is one of the primary brain areas driving our instinctual responses. We have two amygdalae contained deep within the temporal lobes and they connect to the underside of our frontal lobes involved in regulating our emotions.

The amygdala quickly screens and evaluates incoming information. It is also involved in the expression of our core emotions. When we recoil at the sight of a snake in the garden only to realize it was only a piece of old garden hose, it was the amygdala that helped to prime us for action.

The infamous fear response that causes so many people to lose money by acting hastily and irrationally is also linked to instinctual decisions based on the amygdala. The fear of loss can be seen in the eyes of your fellow investors and in response to rapidly declining prices. The collapsing narrative that appears to be going astray can extend this fear response. Acting on instinct with an engaged fight or flight response is no way to consistently make money. We need to deploy methods to guard against fear taking over.

Intuition

Intuition occupies the middle level of the pyramid in Figure 2.1. It is characterized by well-learned and relatively automatic responses. Intuitive responses require little attention, but are not as automatic as instincts. Intuition involves more complex mental representations than our instincts, but we don't have much conscious access to intuitive judgments, or where they come from. Just as an expert chess player has a wide array of intuitive moves that can be quickly deployed with little active attention, finance experts make rapid, low effort, intuitive decisions based on what they have experienced repeatedly.

Intuition is facilitated by the brain's reward and punishment learning systems. The basal ganglia are a set of brain structures that guide our intuitive level of thinking with the help of a neurotransmitter chemical called *dopamine*. Neurophysiologist, Wolfram Schultz, and his colleagues discovered important reward responses by recording active basal ganglia neurons in awake, behaving monkeys.[2] Schultz presented random sounds, or visual cues to the monkeys, who then received a rewarding squirt of liquid. The monkey's basal ganglia neurons spiked vigorously just after the liquid was delivered. Next, the monkey learned that a

---

[2]   Schultz, W., P. Dayan, and P.R. Montague. 1997. "A Neural Substrate of Prediction and Reward." *Science* 275, no. 5306, pp. 1593–1599.

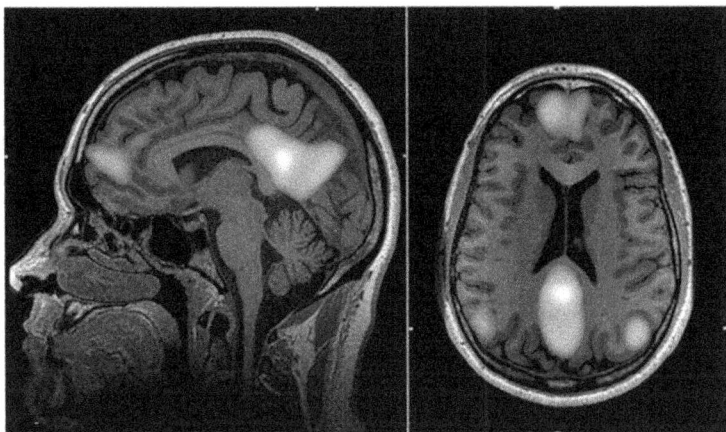

Figure 2.2 The default mode network regions of the brain.

Source: Public domain image from wikimedia commons

particular sound or image *predicted* the reward and the dopamine neurons began to spike when that cue was presented, rather than the actual reward. In other words, these neurons are critical for learning. In this case, the basal ganglia moved from signaling the reward itself toward predicting the future reward.

Intuitive, learned responses are made possible by the basal ganglia. Brain imaging studies have shown us that people activate these areas in response to money and activity in this area appears to guide our behavior quickly and automatically.[3] Such responses may represent our hunches. Our intuition is highly subject to cognitive bias, as we act without fully thinking through the consequences and make use of less information than is actually available to us.

Intuitive thinking is supported by the midline areas between the hemispheres in both the frontal lobes and parietal lobes (Figure 2.2). Brain activity moves inward toward these midline areas when we are awake, but not particularly attentive to the world around us. Brain researchers call this type of activity the *default mode* network, as it is linked to general

---

[3] McClure, S.M., M.K. York, and P.R. Montague. 2004. "The Neural Substrates of Reward Processing in Humans: The Modern Role of FMRI." *The Neuroscientist* 10, no. 3, pp. 260–268.

wakefulness without being engaged in a mentally demanding task.[4] Krawczyk's research has linked activity in these areas to *framing bias*, which we describe in the next chapter.[5]

We make intuitive decisions in investing because they just *feel right*. Without our awareness, our basal ganglia may be guiding us toward making particular decisions. We make intuitive responses rapidly and effortlessly throughout our day. As with instinct-based responses, intuitions can lead us astray when we act impulsively. Unlike instinct responses, which are often only suited toward very short-term choices, our intuitions can be highly effective in investment analysis, particularly as our expertise builds.

Reason

At the top of the inverted pyramid (Figure 2.1) is *reason*, which requires effort and demands our attention. Reasoning deals with complex information and requires mental work to think through a situation carefully. These characteristics make reasoning slower than the other levels. You engage your powers of reason when you develop an investment narrative. Careful analysis is all about analyzing trends, making active comparisons among companies, and considering multiple factors, such as competitive position, cyclicality, management, and industry dynamics. Reason divides into two sub-categories: our *internal thinking* and our *external thinking*.

Internal thinking involves letting our minds wander and running through mental simulations of possibilities. This can involve directing attention inward and comparing our current thoughts on a position with previous information from the past. The *default mode network* supports this type of reflective thinking and our intuition (Figure 2.2). It is

---

[4] Fox, M.D., A.Z. Snyder, J.L. Vincent, M. Corbetta, D.C. Van Essen, and M.E. Raichle. 2005. "The Human Brain is Intrinsically Organized into Dynamic, Anticorrelated Functional Networks." *Proceedings of the National Academy of Sciences* 102, no. 27, pp. 9673–9678.

[5] Murch, K.B., and D.C. Krawczyk. 2013. "A Neuroimaging Investigation of Attribute Framing and Individual Differences." *Social Cognitive and Affective Neuroscience* 9, no. 10, pp. 1464–1471.

a metaphorical coincidence that directing our attention inward toward our own personal thoughts moves our brain activity inward toward the middle of the two hemispheres. Internal evaluations require mental effort and focused attention unlike intuitive responses, which sometimes also involve the default mode network. These evaluations also activate several other networked brain areas involved in emotion, visual imagery, and semantic meaning depending on where our internal thoughts guide us.

Investors frequently focus on external information. We attend to new information on a position and make active comparisons between indicators, consider recent pricing trends, and make sense of our colleagues' thoughts on a position. This type of reasoning is supported by a set of areas known as the *task network* (Figure 2.3). This network supports our focus on incoming information and consists of the lateral frontal and lateral parietal lobes. Maintaining and manipulating incoming information moves brain activity outward toward the edges of the hemispheres. In other words, moving your focus toward the outside environment drives activity toward the outer portions of the cortex—which is easy to remember.

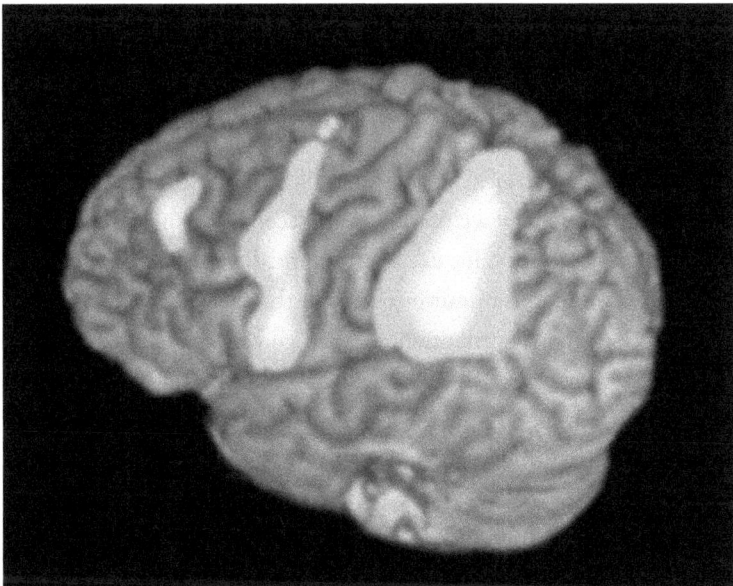

Figure 2.3 Task mode network regions of the brain

Simply engaging your brain's default mode and task networks is not enough to overcome behavioral biases. Avoiding biases requires us to set in place plans and procedures that guide us to attend to much of the information that we often neglect once we become fixated on particular aspects of a narrative. Careful thinking at the reason level offers a remedy to biased analysis. We will focus on specific strategies to enhance your reasoning in Chapter 8.

> *It is useless to attempt to reason a man out of a thing he was never reasoned into.*
>
> —Jonathan Swift

Switching On the Juice!

Your Norepinephrine System in Action

How do our brains "know" whether to engage in reason, intuition, or just wing it relying on instinct? The answer lies primarily within one critical factor: *context.* "Context determines everything." "It's not what you say, but how you say it." "An image is worth a thousand words." "This isn't the time, or the place" you get the idea. Context makes or breaks us.

> *Nice try kid, but I think you just brought a knife to a gunfight.*
>
> —Indiana Jones

The brain is highly attuned to adapting to the context during new situations, but unfortunately we become complacent over time. To overcome this complacency, our brains use a secret ingredient called *norepinephrine* (NE). This is a neurotransmitter chemical that allows you to switch on your attention. As your attention ebbs, so goes your focus. A brain area called the *locus coeruleus* (LC) is involved in activating the NE system, in effect "turning on the juice" and calling our deliberative, outward-focused, task network into action.[6]

---

[6]   Aston-Jones, G., and J.D. Cohen. 2005. "An Integrative Theory of Locus Coeruleus-Norepinephrine Function: Adaptive Gain and Optimal Performance." *Annu. Rev. Neurosci.* 28, pp. 403–450.

There is a simple biological marker of locus coerulous-norepinephrine (LC-NE) system action: pupil dilation. LC-NE activity is related to the size of your pupils at any given moment. In this case, the eye really is a window to the soul for gauging the thinking style that we are using.

Take a moment to answer the following math questions:

1. What's 2 + 2?
2. What's 5 x 5?
3. What's 336 x 3?

If we had installed a webcam to secretly monitor your pupil size as you solved these problems, there would likely have been almost no change in your pupils when you solved Questions 1 and 2. The answers are so well rehearsed that we produce them quickly and intuitively—no NE needed.

When you tried to answer Question 3, you likely had to engage your task network, orient your attention toward the incoming information, and effortfully churn through the numbers to produce the answer. As you estimated the workload and began the mental calculation, our secret webcam would likely have detected a rapid dilation of your pupils, the marker of LC-NE activity. The NE signal helps to focus our frontal lobes toward sustaining our attention. In effect, pupil size signals a move from intuitive thinking to reasoning.

This remarkable pupil finding was initially discovered by iconic behavioral bias researcher, Daniel Kahneman and his colleague, Jackson Beatty in the 1960s.[7] Later research has confirmed that pupil dilation can be an effective marker of thinking style and is related to individual differences in cognition. Attention, memory, and reasoning performance have all been linked to the ability to dilate our pupils and sustain our attention to get things done.[8]

So why don't we just turn on the LC-NE system all the time, use reasoned analysis, and become immune to intuitive and instinctual cognitive

---

[7] Kahneman, D., and J. Beatty. 1966. "Pupil Diameter and Load on Memory." *Science* 154, no. 3756, pp. 1583–1585.

[8] Beatty, J. 1982. "Task-Evoked Pupillary Responses, Processing Load, and the Structure of Processing Resources." *Psychological Bulletin* 91, no. 2, p. 276.

biases? Unfortunately, this is not possible, as the LC-NE system fatigues after some time. This LC-NE fatigue accompanies the inevitable boredom and mind wandering that eventually follow bouts of mental effort. How do you get the next NE jolt to regain your reasoning edge? Again, *context* is the answer. New and engaging situations stimulate the LC-NE system. This re-establishes our deliberative reasoning, clicking our task networks back into high gear.

Notice that if context is the key, then we can creatively alter our context through best practices that ensure that we minimize instinctive and intuitive biases, as well as those that emerge when we reason. As we cover each bias, we will walk you through methods that you can put in place to avoid cognitive biases at each of the three levels. We will revisit all of these best practices and offer general recommendations in Chapter 8.

General stress activates the locus coeruleus, from which noradrenergic neurons project to many areas around the brain. A key result of this activation is increased attentiveness to the outside world.

—changingminds.org

Take Away Message

A brain network view of investing: Now that we have established that the brain manages different information via multiple systems, how do these systems work together and what does this tell us about investing in action? Let's consider what happens to our brain's attention systems during investment behaviors.

(a) When you look for an attractive opportunity, you may initially be drawn to certain salient features. This is the LC-NE system in action prompting your brain to engage the position at the *reason* level. You generate a sound basis for why a position is currently undervalued. Your task network activates as you use your external focus of attention to evaluate the different factors relevant to establishing the value of the company. The LC-NE system helps to tune your frontal neurons to sustain attention on your analysis. You can willfully control your attention as you think through management behavior, recent news, industry trends, and earnings trends. The task network helps you to sketch out a mental model of the position. This is a rough sketch; however, there is more work to do to produce a reasoned analysis of the position.

(b) You now begin to think through the position in relation to your prior knowledge using the default mode network in concert with memory-related neurons. This process allows you to fill in details to predict how things will likely play out. You can reference similar companies that you have analyzed in the past, and begin to flesh out your narrative by combining internally generated theories with externally gathered evidence using your powers of reason. Ultimately, you can embellish upon and clarify the rough sketch model and better predict the future performance of the company. After you complete your analysis, you initiate a position.

(c) Working with your fleshed out narrative, you monitor the price and watch minor gains and losses. When the price rises your default mode network activity is sustained. Dopamine neurons in the basal ganglia begin to move your attention toward incoming information that predicts a price increase. Things continue to develop in your favor and you begin to gain confidence about the position. Your frontal lobes churn through the incoming data about the business and you continue to receive small bits of good news as returns mount. There is no reason to change course right now, as your narrative seems to be playing out successfully. Soon your mind wanders toward thoughts of selling for healthy returns. This is a key point at which we can fall victim to bias, since the narrative and ongoing events match, potentially leading us to become complacent.

(d) After several weeks pass, trouble is brewing. Gains start to slow down. Unexpected dips in price grab your attention stoking up the LC-NE system. Your brain moves from default mode activity to task network activation when you think about this position and reason through the sudden gaps between your narrative and the incoming pricing data. You focus attention and seek new information as the data begin to turn against your narrative. Your brain focuses on learning from changes in relevant factors as you consider what might be going on. The basal ganglia begin to fire error signals indicating that expected gains are suddenly missing. As these signals continue, your frontal lobes move into a learning mode. Your networks are regaining flexibility to enable you to somehow adapt to regain an edge on this position.

(e) The instinct level takes over as your amygdala begins to activate as losses mount and bad news continues. Your brain moves into a fear mode as threat signals move you toward the brink of panic. The position is collapsing and you may need to sell and try to avoid major losses.

(f) With your internal reason system, you struggle to get your emotions under control and focus on sticking with the position despite the bad news. Things have to turn around, as you believe your initial reasoning was sound. How could you have been wrong? What can you possibly do to turn things around?

This example above leads us into the next chapter, in which we will walk you through many of the most prominent attention-related cognitive biases that can lead a sound investor astray.

You can't depend on your eyes when your imagination is out of focus.
—Mark Twain

Summary

- We have multiple modes of thinking at our disposal. Three key modes in investing are *instinct, intuition,* and *reasoning*.
- Thinking modes are supported by different brain networks. Instinct is linked to the amygdala. Intuition is linked to the default mode network and basal ganglia. Reason is linked to the task network (external thinking), the default mode network (internal thinking), as well as areas specialized in language, perception, and memory.
- The context is especially important for determining which of the thinking styles we will use during a particular situation.

- Many cognitive biases result from failures to engage in reasoned analysis (either external or internal) along with overreliance on intuition and instinct.
- The LC system operates with NE, a chemical messenger that arouses our attention and engages the task network to facilitate reasoned analysis.
- Investing requires attention toward internal and external information supported by strong reliance on the task network and our reasoning ability.
- To invest wisely, we must master control over our instincts and put processes in place that limit over-reliance on intuition.

Overconcentration on any one point is distortion.

—Camille Paglia

Recommended Additional Readings

Fuster, J.M. 2003. *Cortex and Mind: Unifying Cognition.* Oxford University Press.
Kahneman, D. 2011. *Thinking, Fast and Slow.* Macmillan.

CHAPTER 3

Attention Biases Described

I. Focused Attention Biases

Attention requires us to elevate preferred information, while suppressing all other information. Accomplishing this requires the brain to constantly engage in separating out signal from noise. Many times we succeed in attending to the right things; the sights, sounds, and actions that help us attain our goals. We screen out all of the other irrelevant possibilities. Amid these successes, we experience some failures of attention; times when we focus on the wrong information and begin to screen out critical features. Some of these cognitive errors happen consistently across many individuals. This chapter focuses on biases driven by failures of our brain's attention systems.

As discussed in Chapter 2, we can engage information at different levels (instinct, intuition, and reason). At the *reason* level we can direct our attention toward internal information, such as mental models and prior knowledge, or focus externally on incoming information, and make active comparisons between our mental models and what is actually occurring. By contrast, we have little control of our attention when we operate at the *instinct* level, as this is a fast, automatic, and reflexive style. *Intuition* also leaves us with less control of our attention. Many of the attention biases span the intuition and reason levels, and are marked by failures to attend to key information, while we devote too much attention toward other information. This results in distorted thinking that can undermine financial performance.

In this chapter, we will define each bias, discuss the relevant research, illustrate it with examples, describe it in terms of its level(s) of processing, and discuss brain mechanisms relevant to its emergence. We will also identify investing styles that leave us most open to experiencing each of the biases. Lastly, we will highlight some important remedies relevant to each bias. These will also be more fully covered in Chapter 8. Understanding the attention biases can help you to implement bias-reduction strategies that target and eliminate common challenges to financial performance.

Salience Bias

Definition: Some things grab our attention more than others. This clearly applies to sights and sounds, but it also applies to ideas. The *salience bias* is a tendency to pay particular attention to prominent information over less obvious information.

Background: The salience bias has been investigated in social psychology, economics, and business. Psychologist, Rebecca Collins, and her colleagues, investigated the effect of salience on attitudes about juvenile crime.[1] When people were provided with more extreme and colorful descriptions of crimes, they perceived the messages to be more interesting and persuasive. This suggests that the language used to describe particular factors in an investment may amplify its apparent relevance. Even if we are not influenced by salience ourselves, we may miscalculate the effect of vividly described information on others by over-estimating the degree to which the market will respond to how a particular event is described in the media.

Relevance: Salience bias can be particularly problematic when high profile news coverage about a company is released. News is crafted to grab headlines, so it tends toward hyperbole. Over-emphasizing dramatic events will affect prices, but troublesomely, a sound narrative can become corrupted by fixating too much on new emotional information. This may lead you away from attending to more mundane indicators that are actually more strongly linked to the health of a company and indicative of it's value.

Salience bias is particularly important when we consider news coverage about new developments. For example, Equifax (NYSE: EFX)

---

[1]   Collins, R.L., S.E. Taylor, J.V. Wood, and S.C. Thompson. 1988. "The Vividness Effect: Elusive or Illusory?" *Journal of Experimental Social Psychology* 24, no. 1, pp. 1–18.

suffered a major data breach in 2017 that resulted in the misappropriation of over 140 million people's sensitive personal information. The financial news media posted extreme headlines such as Bloomberg's *"Equifax Hack Exposes Peril of Credit Bureau Model"* and CNBC's *"Equifax will not survive fallout from massive breach, says technology attorney."* And perhaps greatest of all, New York Senate Minority Leader Chuck Schumer described the breach as "one of the most egregious examples of corporate malfeasance since Enron." All of these statements sensationalized the circumstances surrounding the event. Senator Schumer made the connection to Enron, which ultimately ended in bankruptcy. In the context of this news cycle Equifax's stock dropped 35 percent from about $140 per share to around $90 per share. However, if we look at prior large breaches including Anthem and Target where 78 and 70 million customers respectively were hacked, the total costs for each were less than $300 million. If we assume that EFX suffers $1 billion in damages that would be significantly more per customer hacked than in either the Anthem or Target cases, the amount of incremental cost would only equate to about eight dollars per share. As time passed, and the story faded from the headlines the stock gradually recovered to trade at over $120 per share. The data breach cost Equifax, but it was nowhere near the dire state portrayed by the media.

Dramatic headlines get attention and cause the masses to consume news stories and listen to politicians. The effect of the salience bias caused by these stories can create opportunities for levelheaded, observant investors if they can rationally consider the risk of the matter at hand.

Processing Level: Salience bias operates primarily when we think at the intuition level. Instinct can also drive this bias, particularly when emotional events unfold.

Brain Mechanisms: Salience bias arises from the contrast levels present among competing sources of information. Our brains are geared to focus on rich, high-contrast stimuli. Just as a sudden crack of thunder dramatically breaks the silence of a quiet night, colorful and dramatic ideas stand out amid the daily flow of more mundane information. Salience can lead to a norepinephrine surge to boost our attention leading to greater task-mode lateral frontal and parietal lobe activity (see Chapter 2). This bias involves inappropriately amplifying the salient information. As information gathers on a given investment position, the most salient information can start to bias our thinking. As this snowballs, we can end up neglecting important facts.

Who's vulnerable? Novice investors may also be particularly prone to experiencing salience bias.

Remedies:

- Develop a pre-mortem analysis assigning probabilities to potential scenarios that may result in a positive, or negative outcome. The pre-mortem will help you to prevent fear (at the instinct level) from pulling you into reactivity. As you review your pre-mortem, try to statistically quantify the effect of any new information and consider adjusting your initial estimate of the probabilities and impact of the various contingencies that you had assigned early on. This will allow you to question the probable impact of the current development.

- Consider other analogous situations when a salient issue arises.

- Step away from emotional events. Salience bias can be overcome by a calm, careful consideration of the facts at hand. You may want to take a walk, meditate, or sleep before acting on a hastily made decision.

- Pick up a ten-year-old newspaper. It is often helpful to look at similar circumstances that have occurred in the past and what the impacts were. Most likely, much of the financial coverage will be de-coupled from what actually transpired in markets around that timeframe.

- Selectively choose to ignore all news on a position, thereby eliminating many distortions driven by media reports geared toward over-statement.

- It is also helpful to remind yourself that it is in the media's interest to evoke the maximum emotional response. If the severity of the facts and statistics don't align with the intensity of the media banter and the magnitude of a securities price movement, then it often makes sense to invest in the *opposite direction.*

Headlines, in a way, are what mislead you because bad news is a headline, and gradual improvement is not.

—Bill Gates

Default Effect

Definition: The *default effect* describes a situation in which we avoid taking action and stick with the present state of affairs. This can have a dramatic impact upon major decisions in finance and in life.

Background: Experimental psychologists, Laura Kressel and Gretchen Chapman conducted a study of preferences toward end-of-life medical treatments.[2] They asked people to evaluate how much they would want treatments such as antibiotics, surgery, and artificial feeding. Individuals in the experiment were provided with an initial statement indicating a default to either provide treatment, or withhold it. Remarkably, people expressed a significantly stronger preference for end-of-life treatments when given the default to provide treatment compared to the withhold treatment default! One would imagine that a topic this significant should not be influenced by the wording of the default option. Does this apply in real life?

Economists, Brigitte Madrian and Dennis Shea evaluated default wordings upon people's choices regarding 401(k) retirement accounts.[3] They found that people were much more likely to participate in a retirement plan when automatic enrollment was the default option. Additionally, a large number of people who opted into automatic enrollment chose to keep the default contribution rates and fund allocations. Strikingly, many people become immobilized once a decision has presented itself. Perhaps this bias toward the status quo is linked to people's tendency toward loss aversion. When you are locked in on a situation, you tend

---

[2]   Kressel, L.M., and G.B. Chapman. 2007. "The Default Effect in End-of-Life Medical Treatment Preferences." *Medical Decision Making* 27, no. 3, pp. 299–310.
[3]   Madrian, B.C., and D.F. Shea. 2001. "The Power of Suggestion: Inertia in 401 (k) Participation and Savings Behavior." *The Quarterly Journal of Economics* 116, no. 4, pp. 1149–1187.

to favor staying with it, even when the reasons for that initial position are weak.

Relevance: This default bias can creep into our investment behavior. Have you ever held an investment position where you had reached your price target, or your narrative had played out, and the stock drifted in a range for weeks, but you still did nothing? Alternatively, have you ever been in the situation where your thesis was not playing out as you had anticipated, and the stock just went sideways, but you continued to hold the position? In both circumstances, this inaction is characteristic of the default effect.

The default bias is a common problem in portfolio management in part because common investment wisdom emphasizes patience, tax efficiency, and a long-term investment horizon. In many circumstances, inaction is appropriate provided it is consistent with your investment strategy; however, for investments in lower quality or cyclical businesses that are catalyst driven, being asleep at the switch can be very costly. According to a study conducted by JP Morgan in 2014, the median stock return in the Russell 3000 since inception in 1984, was 54 percent *less* than the average return of the index and 40 percent of all stocks in the index had negative absolute returns through 2014.[4] Though the indices rise over time, the median stock tends to drastically underperform the average stock. For this reason, it is important to be mindful and diligent about the execution of your investment strategy for each particular investment.

Processing Level: The default effect operates primarily at the *intuition* level. Instinct can also prevent us from taking a risk and stepping away from the present status quo.

Brain Mechanisms: Our brains have developed some common patterns that help us to manage large amounts of information. When complicated choices (such as fund allocations) are pre-set for us, people often opt to do less work and trust that this default response will probably work out. This has two important effects. First, our brain capacity is freed up, so we have more attention available to work on other complex processing

---

[4]   Morgan, J.P. 2014. "The Agony and the Ecstacy: the Risks and Rewards of a Concentrated Stock Position." *Eye on the Market.* Michael Cembalest.

problems. Second, we can avoid the painful feeling of loss associated with changing course only to find out that we have actively taken more risk than we should have. It hurts to lose, and these losses sting more when we have actively sought them out after leaving our initial position. Prudent investing requires questioning your choices, doing active work, and ensuring that you do not simply lapse into default choices that result in lost opportunities.

Who's vulnerable: Growth investors looking for longer-term gains, Growth with a catalyst investors may also fall victim to the default effect.

Remedies:

- Enact stop-loss techniques. The math of stop losses is pretty simple. If you lose 10 percent on a position then you only need to make 11 percent to recover the loss. If you lose 20 percent, you have to make roughly 25 percent to recover. Finally, if you lose 50 percent you have to make 100 percent to make up the difference. If you have a rule in place to cut your losses at certain levels, it can help you to overcome the default effect. A similar outcome can be achieved by tax loss selling at the end of the year.

- Reconstruct your entire portfolio periodically on paper after you have reviewed the rationale for each of your positions. This will allow you to answer the question "If I did not have this position on today, would I put it on and if so how large would I make it." Addressing this question can be an enlightening exercise and can help you get over otherwise difficult barriers created by the inertia of the status quo.

- Quality matters. When you hold a low quality company that has been rising, it probably just caught a wave. Price will likely undergo mean reversion and you stand to lose a lot. Alternatively, if it is a high quality company, don't worry about it. Warren Buffett has held some companies for decades garnering remarkable returns.

*Also see *optimism bias*

I just wanted to be a composer; I became an actor by default, really.
I got a scholarship to a college of music and drama, hoping to take a
scholarship in music. But I ended up as an acting student, so I've stuck
with that for the last 50-odd years.

—Anthony Hopkins

Optimism Bias

Definition: While most investors will not make money during the next
economic downturn, you will come out ahead. Sounds appealing, right?
People tend to be unrealistically optimistic about the future. The *optimism bias* leads people to fixate on positive feedback and neglect negative feedback. We are more likely to upgrade our predictions based
on positive feedback that our given narrative is correct. We also tend
to fail to adjust our predictions sufficiently in response to negative
information.

Background: The optimism bias has been observed in a variety of contexts
in the scientific literature. Social psychologist, Neil Weinstein, illustrated
this robust bias as people evaluated both positive and negative information.[5] Weinstein reported that people estimated their chances of obtain-
ing higher salaries than their peers by as much as 40 percent, a clear case
of unrealistically evaluating positive information. He also reported that
people are much less likely to endorse the possibility that they will con-
tract a life threatening illness than others, a case of inappropriately downgrading negative information.

Other studies have also revealed optimism bias. Researchers found
that people believed they were more likely to pay off student loans quickly
and obtain higher salaries relative to their peers.[6] Furthermore, those with
the highest level of student debt were guilty of the greatest unfounded
optimism! Animal researchers have reported that even birds and rats

---

[5]   Weinstein, N.D. 1980. "Unrealistic Optimism about Future Life Events."
Journal of Personality and Social Psychology 39, no. 5, p. 806.
[6]   Seaward, H.G., and S. Kemp. 2000. "Optimism Bias and Student Debt." *New
Zealand Journal of Psychology* 29, no. 1, pp. 17–19.

are guilty of the optimism bias by favoring actions linked to preferable outcomes under ambiguous circumstances.[7] This last class of findings suggests that the optimism bias is especially difficult to ignore and may be directly related to the foraging capacity of our brains (refer to basal ganglia activity as discussed in Chapter 2).

A good way to overcome optimism bias is by playing poker. Players are often tempted to continue to play in losing hands because they feel that they are "winners." Each of us is the hero of our own story and the hero typically wins. However, in poker the cards are what they are and no one is special. If you approach the game with the notion that you are destined to win, you will soon come to realize that is not the case. In other words, poker is humbling. The investment markets are no different. It is just better to learn the lesson with stakes that are much smaller than your investment dollars.

Relevance: The optimism bias can have clear negative consequences, as investors overweight the likelihood of desirable outcomes of their investment decisions. Unfortunately, every investment decision involves some degree of risk and with risk comes the possibility of loss. We all imagine that we will be successful in our investments. Despite our feelings of uniqueness, the market is indifferent, similar to the poker table. Those who fall victim to the optimism bias may ignore risk and inappropriately size their positions. There have been many intelligent investors who have "blown up" because of their overly optimistic outlook, which caused them to ultimately take too much risk. This is perhaps most dramatically illustrated when leverage is involved. Warren Buffett once put it well when he said, "leverage is how smart people go broke." If an investor consistently takes large levered bets, then he or she may get lucky and succeed tremendously a few times. If they persist with that investment approach over a prolonged period, ultimately they will blow up when the odds are not in their favor.

Optimism bias is also often pervasive among company management teams. This is particularly the case with CEOs. The CEO of an

---

[7]   Roelofs, S., H. Boleij, R.E. Nordquist, and F.J. van der Staay. 2016. "Making Decisions Under Ambiguity: Judgment Bias Tasks for Assessing Emotional State in Animals." *Frontiers in Behavioral Neuroscience* 10, p. 119.

organization has to inspire those around them, so optimism is often a pre-
requisite of the job. As leaders, they have to be able to convince their team
to "charge the hill" even when the circumstances look quite bleak. It can
be a risk to listen to the CEO because you may find yourself adopting
their narrative about the company's prospects without properly evaluating
these for yourself.

Processing Level: The optimism bias is an *intuition* bias. We are frequently
guided by a feeling that things will work out in the end, even when available evidence suggests otherwise.

Brain Mechanisms: This bias is rooted within the prediction systems of
our brains. Our brains constantly process information related to obtain-
ing rewards and avoiding punishments. We make predictions about the
future based on these unfolding reward/punishment histories. The problem is that we tend to over-estimate the chances of future positive outcomes relative to their actual probability.

Neuroscientist, Tali Sharot and her colleagues, asked people about their
tendency to experience illnesses relative to the population overall.[8] When
negative personal outcomes were presented, people often failed to adjust their
assessments based on this unexpectedly dire information. This insensitivity
to negative outcomes was linked to activity within the right frontal lobe.
Meanwhile, people tended to track positive information about the future
quite well and these predictions were related to left frontal lobe activity.

Who's vulnerable: All investors are likely to face challenges from the optimism bias, as it is a deeply human tendency.

Remedies:

- While people think they are the heroes of the story, remember
  the universe does not care! Sit down at a poker table and you
  quickly realize that you aren't all that special and all the mys-
  tical powers of nature cannot stop you from getting bad cards
  just about as often as the next hero or heroine. Remember
  that the same principle applies to your investing.
- Engage your internal powers of reason and actively remind
  yourself that you may be wrong in your analysis.

---

[8] Sharot, T., A.M. Riccardi, C.M. Raio, and E.A. Phelps. 2007. "Neural Mechanisms Mediating Optimism Bias." *Nature* 450, no. 7166, p. 102.

- Seek criticism from others. Don't get complacent. Try publishing position details and you will get feedback from others—and be reminded that you are just one of many people striving to figure out the future on a given position.
- Seek out a Devil's advocate. Possibly force yourself to attend to clues about negativity on your position (this is especially relevant for a position you are confident about).

*Also see *ostrich effect*

Optimism is the madness of insisting that all is well when we are miserable.

—Voltaire

Ostrich Effect

Definition: Good news inspires us, while bad news deflates us. The *ostrich effect* biases us to ignore bad news, like the proverbial ostrich sticking its head in the sand. This bias is problematic, as it skews attention away from information that may be critical. As we ignore negative news, we also run the risk of paying too much attention to positive reports, analyses, or trends, thereby compounding the problem by placing too much weight on the positive and badly misjudging our position.

Background: Niklas Karlsson and his colleagues reported on the Ostrich effect in 2009.[9] He and his colleagues had predicted that investors would vary in the number of times that they chose to look up information on their fund performance according to previous average returns for the OMXSPI index. Using electronic index data, they found that people did indeed avoid looking up the performance of their funds, especially after bad market index news relative to just after a market increase. This suggests that investors may choose to ignore the pain associated with bad news.

Relevance: Typically, the ostrich effect takes place when bad news or market dynamics turn unfavorable for a previous winner. With respect to sell-side

---

[9] Karlsson, N., G. Loewenstein, and D. Seppi. 2009. "The Ostrich Effect: Selective Attention to Information." *Journal of Risk and Uncertainty* 38, no. 2, pp. 95–115.

favorites that brokers have touted to their clients, there are strong incentives to gloss over problems that are inconsistent with their previously bullish bias. This occurs when the market shifts or when a company produces it's first bad quarter. Typically, companies will stretch to exceed consensus estimates. When quarters are missed it usually signals the beginning of a bad trend. Studies have shown that company management teams regularly engage in earnings management to meet quarterly earnings expectations.[10] You have to start with the assumption that every company manages its earnings. This can be done legally by decreasing discretionary spending, delaying new projects, booking revenues now rather than in the next quarter, providing incentives for customers to pull more sales forward, postponing accounting charges, repurchasing shares, or making other discretionary accounting assumptions. So if a company misses earnings, you have to assume that they have pulled every lever they can legally pull to make the number. This indicates that the first miss is likely the beginning of a new trend. As one CFO put it, "If you see one cockroach, you immediately assume that there are hundreds behind the walls, even though you may have no proof that this is the case."[11] As a consequence, when a company misses earnings for the first time in several quarters it is dangerous to ignore it, but many investors and analysts persist is discounting the bad news as noise.

Processing Level: The ostrich effect is an *intuitive* bias, but may also be influenced by *instinct* if news in particularly dire and emotional.

Brain Mechanisms: The ostrich effect moves our focus of attention inappropriately away from key information that happens to be negative and unsettling. The attention systems of the brain do too good a job of screening out the negative information. This phenomenon can occur implicitly, when we become attached to an investment position and systematically discount information that runs counter to our thesis. This effect may also take place explicitly, when an investor becomes uncomfortable and emotional in the presence of negative news, so she therefore actively shuts it out as a coping mechanism. Either situation can be harmful to your portfolio. The brain's default mode network dominates thinking on the

---

[10]   Graham, J.R., C.R. Harvey, and S. Rajgopal. 2006. "Value Destruction and Financial Reporting Decisions." *Financial Analytics Journal* 62, no. 6, pp. 27–39.
[11]   *Id.*

position and you actively screen incoming information preventing the reasoning task network and from doing its job.

Who's vulnerable: Most investors will have a difficult time calibrating the effects of bad news. This may plague people who have held a position for a long time and have become too psychologically attached to it.

Remedies:

- The ostrich effect leads us to avoid being mindful of news that could affect the narrative surrounding a company. The remedies we look to employ should shake us out of our intellectual slumber so that we can reassess things rationally.

- When bad news surfaces, it helps to get a second opinion. Reach out to a disinterested, yet sophisticated third party who has no interest in the issue. When you do this, try hard not to provide any information about your personal bias, or position. Your colleague's reaction might help you see if this is a problem worth being concerned about.

- Stomp out the cockroaches! When you see one, it means bad news *and* generally that more bad news will soon be coming. A bad earnings report means trouble, as most people will distort as much as possible to make earnings look better than they are. Pay attention to the signs!

- Perform a pre-mortem analysis and look back and review it regularly. Reviewing a position at timed intervals can help to avoid over-attachment and ostrich-like behavior. Revisit your notes after news breaks and consider how it affects your thesis. Did you anticipate the problem in your pre-mortem document? If yes, then you might consider reducing your risk.

*Also see *optimism bias*

> *Don't pay any attention to the critics—don't even ignore them.*
> —Samuel Goldwyn

Framing Bias

Definition: Would you rather have a glass that is half empty, or one that is half full? Information can be described to highlight either its positive, or negative features. People act differently toward negatively framed

information by tending to take greater risks to avoid negative consequences. In other words "It's not what you say, it's how you say it."

Background: The decision-making literature describes several types of
framing effects. Most relevant to finance is *risk framing,* described by
Daniel Kahneman and Amos Tversky.[12] In one of their framing experiments, people were told that a new unknown disease was about to strike
potentially killing 600 people. They were asked to decide between two
disease control options. In one version, people were offered a choice
between a sure thing (400 people will be *saved*), or a gamble in which
there was a 1/3 chance that no one would be *saved* and a 2/3 chance that
everyone would be *saved.* In this positively framed set of plans, people
more often preferred the sure thing (saving 400 people's lives). In a second version, the same plans were offered, this time worded negatively as
a sure thing (200 people will *die*) and a gamble (1/3 chance that everyone
would *die* and a 2/3 chance that no one would *die*). In the negatively
framed version, people tended to prefer the *riskier* second option that
might fail completely. Why choose differently based on the same situation? We often take greater risks to avoid negatively framed consequences
than we otherwise would. Context changes things.

Relevance: Framing effects apply widely in our daily lives. Psychologist,
Irwin Levin, demonstrated that people rate ground beef as being tastier
and higher quality when it is described as being 75 percent lean, compared to when it is claimed to contain 25 percent fat![13] There are many
situations in investing that require risk assessments and any of these may
be subject to undue influence from positive or negative information simply based on how things are framed.

Framing effects are particularly relevant when considering portfolio
management. When investors focus on individual stock decisions, they
often exhibit the *disposition effect,* a well-documented observation that
investors are more willing to sell winning stocks in their portfolio, but
tend to hold on to or add to losers. This tendency often arises from looking

[12]   Kahneman, D., and A. Tversky. 2013. "Choices, Values, and Frames." In
Handbook of the Fundamentals of Financial Decision Making: Part I, pp. 269–278.
[13]   Levin, I.P. 1987. "Associative Effects of Information Framing." *Bulletin of the
Psychonomic Society* 25, no. 2, pp. 85–86.

at individual positions and wanting to avoid a loss on losing stocks and lock in gains on winners.

The great investor, Peter Lynch, once described this practice as follows: "Selling your winners and holding your losers is like cutting the flowers and watering the weeds." The disposition effect imposes substantial costs on investors, who pay more capital gains taxes than necessary. In the short term, companies that outperform the market are likely to continue to do so, while those that underperform will likely continue as well. Investors can mitigate the power of the disposition effect by taking more of a portfolio-wide perspective, rather than focusing on individual positions in isolation. In this context, the losing stocks can be cut in order to mitigate risk and in most instances winners can be held assuming they are quality businesses. In most cases the decision to buy, sell, or hold should be driven by portfolio risk considerations and individual position fundamentals and not by the arbitrary dictates of loss avoidance.

Processing Level: Risk framing often occurs at an *intuition* level, in which we reflexively try to avoid risks. In the case of very high possible losses, we may even experience *instinct*-driven loss avoidance. A reasoned approach is needed to overcome framing effects.

Brain Mechanisms: We conducted a brain imaging study evaluating the brain-basis of the framing effect. In the experiment, people decided differently when they were asked about positively-framed compared to negatively-framed versions of the same statements.[14] We found that several areas within the frontal lobes became more active in association with decisions that overcame the context allowing people to focus on the details of the situation. Meanwhile, the ventral frontal lobe, often associated with emotional processing, was active for evaluations that were guided by the framing of the decision.

Who's vulnerable: Anyone can fall into the trap of framing bias. We need to be especially vigilant to avoid these attention biases based on mere

---

[14]   Murch, K.B., and D.C. Krawczyk. 2013. "A Neuroimaging Investigation of Attribute Framing and Individual Differences." *Social Cognitive and Affective Neuroscience* 9, no. 10, pp. 1464–1471.

descriptions of the same information, especially when we act quickly, or emotionally.

Remedies:

- Try to actively re-frame things in a positive light when you can. See if this changes your risk perspective before making a drastic move that deviates from your standard process.

- Consider an analogy to poker: actively maintain a longer-term perspective (thereby overcoming short term volatility). It's easy to accept that you will get a bad hand from time-to-time. Again, maintain a longer time-frame viewpoint.

- Changing your time-frame perspective will generally make it easier to cope with volatility. Think in terms of the portfolio and not just the individual position level. Risk is much more diversified at the overall portfolio level, thus reducing the emotional influence on one particular position. The ups and downs in an individual stock price tend to be more tolerable when you re-frame and take a portfolio perspective.

- Make sure to keep risk in check by being disciplined about your investing process. Use disciplined process-driven methods whenever possible.

Many of the truths that we cling to depend on our point of view.
—Jedi Master Yoda

Hindsight Bias

Definition: Occurrences appear much more obvious when we think of them in hindsight. This sentiment is referred to as the *hindsight bias:* a common tendency for people to estimate an event as being more probable after it has occurred, than it would have before. This bias explains the common phrase "hindsight is 20/20." We selectively elevate the probability that something would have occurred simply based on what we know to be the case now.

Background: Psychologist, Baruch Fischhoff, memorably demonstrated the power of hindsight by asking people to estimate the outcome of an obscure historical battle.[15] When people estimated the likelihood of four possible outcomes to the conflict, they claimed all were roughly equally likely. After being provided with a statement that one of the four outcomes had actually occurred, people used the benefit of hindsight to estimate that this actually would have been the most probable outcome. People warped their probability estimates to fit the sure outcome that had been provided.

There have been hundreds of scholarly papers documenting instances of people reporting an upwardly biased likelihood of a particular detail after its reported occurrence. Our minds trick us into thinking that whatever has happened was much more likely to have occurred *a priori*.

Relevance: Once events occur, people have a tendency to think that they were nearly inevitable and that other possible alternatives were much less likely. This causes investors to draw inappropriate lessons from experience. Often when evaluating an investment opportunity the odds are in your favor and the investment makes sense based on the risk-weighted return. Unfortunately, sometimes less likely undesirable scenarios occur and well-reasoned investments lose money.

Imagine you are playing blackjack and you have a jack and an eight. The dealer's face up card is a five. You stand pat and the dealer reveals his face down card to be an ace. He takes a hit and gets a three bringing him to 19 and you lose the game. Hindsight bias can lead you to think that you should have known to take another card when your knowledge at the time of the decision to stand pat clearly dictated that it was the right play. The process was good, but the outcome was undesirable. There is nothing to be learned from the undesirable outcome in this case, but hindsight bias leads us to believe taking a hit would have been the superior move.

This bias creeps in when we have incomplete knowledge about some factors and better knowledge about others. For instance, an investor may sell shares in a consumer goods company because he notices that shipping costs have risen precipitously and that the company's products are starting to face stiff competition from new market entrants. The investor's

[15] Fischhoff, B. 1975. "Hindsight is Not Equal to Foresight: The Effect of Outcome Knowledge on Judgment Under Uncertainty." *Journal of Experimental Psychology: Human Perception and Performance* 1, no. 3, p. 288.

decision may seem less sound in retrospect if the company is later acquired by another larger diversified consumer products company at a price substantially higher than the one he received. Again, in this case the decision made was not wrong simply because the outcome was undesirable and there is probably little to learn here. Nonetheless, some investors may investigate further and conclude that they should have known the company was likely to be acquired due to some characteristic that made it particularly attractive. This re-constructionist application of a narrative to describe the logic of past events is a common symptom of hindsight bias. *Processing Level:* Hindsight bias occurs at the *reason* level, when we mistakenly assume a probability to be overly high in retrospect. We are typically consciously aware of the biased probability, but we struggle to avoid skewing our estimates, as we rarely go to the trouble of statistically analyzing alternate possibilities.

Brain Mechanisms: As our brains take in new information, they become tuned toward particular features, especially when these are surprising. This is appropriate much of the time, as we adjust to developing circumstances; however, we sometimes over-emphasize some events that occurred by chance as being major contributors to the outcome. This leads us to screen out probable outcomes that did not happen to occur due to random circumstances. Ultimately, the brain prioritizes information consistent with hindsight and this can skew our narratives undercutting our ability to forecast events. This bias is driven by our internal thinking and likely relies upon the default mode network and other regions associated with internal thinking.

Who's vulnerable: Investors who follow the news a great deal may be more prone to hindsight bias.

Remedies:

- Take pre-emptive steps: conduct a pre-mortem on your position and scope out in detail how you imagine things will likely play out. When something unexpected happens check if you had identified it as a possibility in your pre-mortem analysis. Try to uncover whether missing this event, or failing to predict it, was a mistake or not. If it was not anticipated, then it may have simply been a fluke—which is okay, no process mistake was made.

- If the unanticipated event was potentially foreseeable, then proceed to change paths accepting that we cannot anticipate all possible future events. If it wasn't a mistake in your process, just accept it and move on.
- Limit your news consumption. This will help you to avoid overly fixating on what did occur as having been inevitable.

In the business world, the rearview mirror is always clearer than the windshield.

—Warren Buffett

In-Group Bias

Definition: We prefer the ideas of those who appear similar to ourselves. We like people more if they are part of our in-group. We give them the benefit of the doubt and we are more likely to cooperate with them. This *in-group bias* can influence our investing choices and the decisions we make about our money.

Background: Our ancestors were tribe members who lived their lives divided into groups. Tribalism is a human tendency creating in-groups and out-groups. The in-group bias has a strong influence on how we evaluate people's personal characteristics. This can have a clear effect on our evaluation of a company's management and image. Some companies feel more familiar due to location, management team, or style of branding. Advertisers are keenly aware of the in-group bias and strive to create brands that people identify with. Strong branding can create a bias toward viewing those loyal to the brand as being part of an in-group. We are more likely to view strangers favorably if they share our brand affinity. When we feel positively toward management, or branding, we may lose sight of the actual operational quality of a company and estimate its price or trajectory to be inappropriately positive.

Relevance: In most instances, you will not make money over time if you follow the crowd. Getting an investing edge requires you to go against the grain and take an action before others have noticed the opportunity. This does not always apply in the short term. During the late 1960s and early 1970s, one could have done well for several years by investing in the popular "nifty 50." In the 1990s buying anything related to the Internet resulted in staggering gains. Since 2013, FAANG (standing for Facebook (NYSE: FB), Apple (Nasdaq: AAPL), Amazon (Nasdaq: AMZN), Netflix (Nasdaq: NFLX), and Google (NASDAQ: GOOG)) stocks have significantly outperformed the market. The problem with following the crowd is that it eventually comes to an end when these stocks become overextended from a valuation perspective. When you invest and everyone agrees, then any change in circumstances can have a drastic effect on the stock in question in the opposite direction of the in-group consensus.

The need to boldly act before others requires that we block the intuitive in-group bias that leads us to follow the herd. Similarly, many investors make poor decisions because they fear missing out on an excellent opportunity. They make a poorly timed purchase because they want to affiliate with the winning team—investors who are sure they are onto a big opportunity.

Listening to expert opinion is another prime example of a case where it can be unwise to follow the crowd. When you identify with an expert's style or analysis, then you may tend to view that person in an overly favorable manner. This can lead to a halo effect, in which you place undue weight upon that person's opinion because you view them as being part of your in-group. Equally insidiously, we may undervalue the opinion of a smart analyst or colleague whom we view as being too different from ourselves. By placing people in an overly familiar or unfamiliar position, we open ourselves toward inappropriate evaluations of their ideas.

Processing Level: Instinct drives us to trust like-minded, similar people. *Intuition* finishes the job by biasing us toward listening to these individuals. *Brain Mechanisms:* The in-group bias emerges from our highly social brains. We quickly identify others as being part of our in-group, probably based on a strong survival instinct that helped our ancient ancestors to reap the benefits of societal behavior.

Neuroscientist, Jay Van Bevel and his colleagues, randomly assigned people of mixed gender and ethnicity to be part of an in-group in a brain imaging experiment.[16] When people viewed faces of these newly

---

[16]   Van Bavel, J.J., D.J. Packer, and W.A. Cunningham. 2008. "The Neural Substrates of In-Group Bias: A Functional Magnetic Resonance Imaging Investigation." *Psychological Science* 19, no. 11, pp. 1131–1139.

assigned in-group members, they activated their orbitofrontal cortex, along with several subcortical areas important for emotion and face recognition. The orbitofrontal cortex is involved in linking emotions and ideas. This area was most strongly related to feelings of liking toward the in-group faces. Such results suggest that the in-group bias is highly automatic and potentially very difficult to overcome. It can inappropriately lead us to attend to some information to the exclusion of other more important details in our evaluation of a company.

Who's vulnerable: Novice investors may be particularly susceptible to the in-group bias if they rely too much on expert opinion. Investors who hold a position for a long duration may also begin to experience this bias. News consumption can also lead you toward viewing the world through the lenses of an in-group member if you begin to adopt a commonly held viewpoint.

Remedies:

- Simply set a policy to avoid investment ideas from others. Consider adopting a "not made here" policy, in which you resist any ideas that you did not originate. Enacting such a policy is a direct way to reduce risk from in-group bias.
- Investing visionary, Benjamin Graham, claimed that the quality of analysis matters most, not what the crowd is doing. Be careful about popularity and about trusting someone else's opinion, or you might inherit their biases. This can be problematic to undo, as you haven't earned the information for yourself leaving you in a challenging position.
- If you are considering another investor's idea, then start off by trying to disprove the idea. This process will give you more ownership of the idea. You will end up better understanding the position through doing the work of evaluation.

See also: hot hand effect, ostrich effect, and *framing bias*

> *To boldly go where no one has gone before.*
>
> —Star Trek, introductory sequence

Hot Hand Effect

Definition: The *hot hand* is a bias that leads us to think that someone who has performed exceptionally well will continue to do so, as they seem to be harnessing some unique capacity at the moment. We may think that such a person is "in the zone" and therefore likely to continue to outdo herself into the future.

Background: During the NBA playoffs this past Spring a CBS news report indicated that the Rockets' Eric Gordon got "hot off the bench," and would "look to keep his hot hand going into the next game."[17] This is such a common commentary in sports reporting that nobody bothers to question it.

The hot hand effect was initially demonstrated by experimental psychologist Thomas Gilovich and his colleagues, who were interested in whether basketball shot making probabilities actually showed increases to support the "hot hand" phenomenon.[18] The researchers analyzed shot-making performance from both NBA teams and college play to determine whether the probability of a given shot being made could be predicted from the shots immediately prior. They found almost no statistical support for the hot hand phenomenon. Their analyses supported a conclusion that sometimes players experience a streak of shots made, but that this is a naturally occurring statistical likelihood, much like getting five or six coins to turn up heads in a row. With enough basketball shots, eventually there will be streaks of one outcome over another, but these are bound to occur by chance alone, not from a mysteriously unexpected burst of skill that can come and go. Furthermore, the researchers found that people's predictions of future success did not track with reality.

Relevance: There is considerable risk when someone expresses a belief in the hot hand effect. This may be particularly true for investors. The hot hand can come in the form of a string of unexpected positive returns.

---

[17] Rockets' Eric Gordon: Gets hot off bench in Game 2 win by RotoWire Staff May 17, 2018.

[18] Gilovich, T., R. Vallone, and A. Tversky. 1985. "The Hot Hand in Basketball: On the Misperception of Random Sequences." *Cognitive Psychology* 17, no. 3, pp. 295–314.

It can also be found in evaluating one's performance. If an analyst has experienced an unexpected (and unearned) run of successful predictions, then he may be given too much credit for those successes and therefore become trusted to an unwise degree. Market environments change over time. Certain investing philosophies or industries can lead to a string of successes, which can make the advocates appear prescient. But then the winds of market favor change and these streaks typically end abruptly. This can be observed today with many guru investment icons whose style was very successful in environments of the past, but have since fallen by the wayside. Those who imitated these gurus by mirroring their investments saw disappointing results.

Processing Level: The hot hand is an *intuitive* bias, which only breaks down when we interrogate a situation with reasoned analysis and statistical methods.

Brain Mechanisms: The hot hand effect stems from times when our brains over-fixate on positive outcomes. The repeated observation of a rewarding success can begin to distort our sense of reality. After a run of successes (that are actually due to chance alone) we can begin to create a narrative that places these successes into a sensible context. The hot hand is related to the *ostrich effect* (this chapter), but in reverse. Instead of actively screening negative information out of the narrative, we artificially attend more toward positive outcomes that fuel a belief in the hot hand. Belief in the hot hand is sustained by our tendency to conclude that we know more than we actually do about a given situation. This can lead to an additional class of unwanted cognitive illusions that we will cover in the next section on cognitive illusions related to attention.

Who's vulnerable? Novice investors are particularly at risk. Beginners tend to be overly trusting of expert opinion. Remember, nobody can *always* pick winners because they may just be experiencing a remarkable streak of luck. In investing, those who possess the most relevant knowledge come out ahead in the long run. Momentum investors may also be tripped up by this bias.

Remedies:

- It's important to look past the advice given by a market prognosticator, or popular stock picker, and conduct your own independent evaluation of each investment thesis. If after

your own investigation it still appears to be a sound idea, then
it might be appropriate for investment.

- It is never wise to make an investment decision following
some brilliant investor or analyst who appears to be "on fire"
without any additional diligence. If you make such a decision,
when will you know that you are wrong? When would be the
right time to take profits? You cannot answer these questions
without doing your own work.

- If you are considering borrowing an idea from someone else,
first try to disprove it. By performing your own evaluation,
you will gain more ownership of the idea and a better understanding of its fundamentals.

*See also: *in-group bias, ostrich effect,* and *framing bias*

Unthinking respect for authority is the greatest enemy of truth.
—Albert Einstein

II. Cognitive Illusions Related to Attention

In this section, we discuss the impact of sustained attention on our subsequent conscious perceptions. Once we have developed a narrative and
start to see evidence of it playing out, we can find ourselves gaining a false
sense of security, becoming over-confident, and taking unwise risks. This
next class of biases stems from interactions between our attention systems
and our conscious beliefs.

Illusion of Control

Definition: We all experience a sense of control in our lives. Perhaps this
is most clear when we engage in well-practiced activities that we reliably
perform well. Our sense of control is linked to our confidence and our
understanding of a situation. Unfortunately, there are many ambiguous
situations, especially in investing, when we believe that we control outcomes more than we actually do. This is known as the *illusion of control,* a
false belief that we can influence outcomes that we cannot.

Background: Psychologists, Lauren Alloy and Lyn Abramson demonstrated the illusion of control using a simple gambling game.[19] They offered people a button that they could press to see if they could cause a light to turn on. On each trial of the experiment they could choose either to press the button or not, and then observe whether the bulb lit after each choice. The participant was paid a quarter if the bulb lit. After many trials, people were asked how much they controlled the light based on their button pressing. People estimated their control as being high when the bulb illuminated often. Conversely, they estimated their control to be lower when the bulb remained unlit on most of the trials. In fact the experiment was rigged so the bulb lit at random and the participants never had any control! A rational decision maker should have reported no control, as the outcomes did not depend on the button at all.

In a second experiment, the researchers asked people to try to avoid financial losses when the bulb lit. This time they estimated less control than when they played for financial gains. These results suggest that we are especially prone to over-estimating our degree of control when we are playing for money and experiencing a lot of successes ... exactly the type of situation that occurs when we hold a stock that is rising day-by-day.

Relevance: The illusion of control typically is most evident in day-to-day trading. Much day-to-day trading is based on noise. It is not all that different than the flashing light bulbs described above. Nonetheless, many investors will spend the entire day during market hours watching tick-by-tick, suffering from the illusion that they can create value through their trading prowess. In reality, for most investors, this is time wasted that could otherwise be spent finding the next attractive investment opportunity through disciplined work.

The illusion of control can also infiltrate investment analysis. Often managers and analysts prefer investment ideas that they originate to those that come from others. This is often because they have a sense that ideas that originate with them are more likely to be successful. To some degree,

---

[19]   Alloy, L.B., and L.Y. Abramson. 1979. "Judgment of Contingency in Depressed and Nondepressed Students: Sadder But Wiser?" *Journal of Experimental Psychology: General* 108, no. 4, p. 441.

this phenomenon stems from the notion that we are all the hero of our own story and the masters of our universe. Again, the universe does not care and any notion that we have the power to shape the outcomes of the investment world is typically just a fanciful illusion.

Everyone makes errors in their assessment at some point. The illusion of control can lead to catastrophic errors, since it pairs seemingly successful performance with a very high degree of confidence that we have the situation figured out. This bias can also lead to reckless risk taking by elevating an investor's self-esteem and sense of skill to overly high levels.

Processing Level: Intuition and *reasoning* guided by our own consciousness generate this illusion. We can think ourselves into being too confident. In the case of this bias, reasoning about actual outside evidence is an appropriate remediation strategy.

Brain Mechanisms: This bias likely stems from our frontal lobes. People who have frontal lobe damage have been shown to be less susceptible to the illusion of control over outcomes.[20] Our foraging circuitry within the basal ganglia are capable of high fidelity tracking of rewards and penalties, but our frontal lobes can interfere by blocking these signals and instead drawing our attention to the accumulation of positive outcomes and increasing wealth. We can then mislead ourselves into overly optimistic false beliefs about our capabilities and future returns.

Who's vulnerable: Any investor who is on a roll and experiencing healthy returns.

Remedies:

- Size positions appropriately. Do not get carried away with your own sense of control and become overconfident.
- Check your assumptions on a regular basis. Learn to recognize when you are on unstable ground by remaining vigilant. If you find yourself bragging to a friend or colleague about a position that you have done significant work on, then you may be overconfident and should reconsider if your positioning is too aggressive.

---

[20] Wolford, G., S.E. Newman, M.B. Miller, and G.S. Wig. 2004. "Searching for Patterns in Random Sequences." *Canadian Journal of Experimental Psychology/ Revue canadienne de psychologie expérimentale* 58, no. 4, p. 221.

- Try to incorporate quantitative methods and structural factors into your analysis of a position. Statistics are your most helpful tool to really determine value.
- Remember that our notion of the "ground truth," or of what is "real" is always actually an incomplete, or distorted model of reality.
- Applying specific rules can help when these lead to an automatic action item. If you apply rules with discipline, then you can reduce the items that require actual deliberation and thereby reduce the chances of falling victim to illusions of control.

* also see *optimism bias* and *hot hand effect*

> *It is far harder to kill a phantom than a reality.*
>
> —Virginia Woolf

Gambler's Fallacy

Definition: This bias is a tendency for people to treat independent events (gambles) as if they depend upon previous outcomes. While smart investing is not the same as a game of chance, this bias can still emerge in economic and financial forecasting.

Background: Bill walked into the Flamingo Hilton to play the slots. It was late morning and the casino was very empty. Despite having his choice of slot machine, Bill made a long walk across the slots area to a row along the wall and insisted on playing the third *Wicked Winnings* machine on the left. He had fruitlessly played this same machine for much of the previous two days and was sure that it was "due to pay out." It had to some time. The *gambler's fallacy* is witnessed daily by countless convenience store clerks who watch many people repeatedly play the same string of lottery numbers sure that they are bound to hit.

The gambler's fallacy was described by influential mathematician Pierre Laplace.[21] It has been demonstrated dozens of times in the

---

21   Laplace, P.S. 1951. *Philosophical Essays on Probabilities*, translated by F.W. Truscott and F. L. Emory. New York, NY: Dover.

behavioral economics and psychology literature. It applies in real life as well. For example, when a particular lottery number occurs people tend to play it less frequently after the win and then gradually it regains popularity.[22] It is as if the occurrence of the number makes it less likely to recur despite its independence on each draw.

Relevance: The gambler's fallacy applies in many instances. Suppose that a stock has been rising. Over time it has continued to rise and despite having no strong evidence one way or another, an investor decides to sell before it goes into the inevitable downturn that is almost sure to follow. We can apply similar faulty thinking to a stock that has been weakly dropping for several months, it's bound to turn around soon, so we better hold on to it. These tendencies arise from an incorrect belief that the performance of a given investment will turn around simply based on previous pricing. An investor guilty of this fallacy acts as if a mysterious general averaging process governs prices and that the future can be prognosticated based on simply watching the price over time.

Processing Level: The gambler's fallacy often represents a failure of *intuition*, in which someone just feels that his or her luck is bound to turn. Perhaps more troublesomely, it can operate at the level of our internally generated *reasoning* when someone genuinely believes that highly improbable events are due to occur soon based on unseen forces.

Brain Mechanisms: The gambler's fallacy likely derives from our brain's reinforcement learning mechanisms. Our incentive processing systems excel at seeking out immediate rewards and rapidly changing course when a strategy is no longer productive. Brain imaging results from Gui Xue, Antoine Bechara, and their colleagues indicated that the frontal and parietal control areas of the brain become more engaged in decisions after losses than after gains.[23] This brain activity is consistent with a tendency to engage in a learning mode in which one attempts to find a new pattern after experiencing ineffective outcomes (see Chapter 2 for details).

---

[22]   Clotfelter, C.T., and P.J. Cook. 1993. "The "Gambler's Fallacy in Lottery Play." *Management Science* 39, no. 12, pp. 1521–1525.

[23]   Xue, G., Z. Lu, I.P. Levin, and A. Bechara. 2011. "An fMRI Study of Risk-Taking Following Wins and Losses: Implications for the Gambler's Fallacy." *Human Brain Mapping* 32, no. 2, pp. 271–281.

Repeating the same gamble because of an over-riding belief that it will eventually work out may arise from a faulty theory that we can anticipate future returns that are bound to happen after repeatedly experiencing losses. This mechanism helps with short-term decisions, but creating an extended narrative based on these feelings is counter-productive.

Who's vulnerable: Novice investors are particularly at risk for the gambler's fallacy. The stock market is not merely a game of chance. Pricing is based largely on company performance and bad companies are not "due to pay out" over time. Likewise, the prices of good companies are not destined to "fall back to Earth" randomly either.

Remedies:

- Do not assume that mean reversion will happen. It will not if you happen to be investing in a poor company. Make sure you really understand timing and the quality of the company you are taking a position in.
- Consider implementing rules-based practices, as these limit your susceptibility to several biases that emerge over time as we think about a position.

Diligence is the mother of good luck.

—Benjamin Franklin

Decision Fatigue

Definition: Some decisions require active thinking about the available options. These effortful decisions consume our mental resources. *Decision fatigue* occurs when we have made numerous decisions and this has taxed our minds. We then make intuitive, poorly thought out choices. Making decisions at the end of a mentally exhausting day may cost us due to our depleted state of mind. We know we've made a lot of choices, so we end up surrendering to mental exhaustion.

Background: One of the authors, Daniel Krawczyk, once had an opportunity to decide on office furniture. He was initially enthusiastic about the process when he arrived at the furniture showroom. He drank an espresso that had been provided and enjoyed the prospect of choosing some unique color schemes and designs for the space. As the available options mounted and he made more decisions, Krawczyk's willpower began to drop. After over an hour of deciding on styles and colors for desks, countertops, chairs, and tables, he found he was no longer very invested in the process. His bloodstream no longer coursing with caffeine, he became disillusioned and found himself making fast, careless decisions between mid-tone taupes, and putty greys, often letting the showroom attendants guide the process. By the end of two hours, he concluded that almost any office chairs in a vaguely beige color would be acceptable and he would be unlikely to even notice the subtleties of the color or model—another unsuspecting victim of decision fatigue.

Decision fatigue occurs when we exert ourselves in active thought and incur an energy cost, much the same as the toll that physical exercise takes on our muscles. For example, social psychologist, Daniel Gilbert and his colleagues asked people to evaluate an emotional person shown in a video.[24] They asked one group of people to actively ignore a series of irrelevant words that appeared at the bottom of the screen during the video, while another group was simply told that the words were not important for their task. The group that had been instructed to exert effort to ignore the words performed more poorly at evaluating the emotional tones of the person in the video, when compared to the group that exerted less effort. This result implies that active cognitive effort reduces our mental resources and can influence other topics that we try to think about while in the depleted state.

Glucose fuels our brain functions. Neurons within our brains consume glucose at higher levels when we engage in active thinking. Research indicates that replenishment of glucose can help to overcome decision fatigue. Matthew Gailliot, Roy Baumeister, and their colleagues conducted a study of blood glucose levels before and after an active self-control task.[25] These researchers asked one group of people to actively ignore

---

[24]   Gilbert, D.T., D.S. Krull, and B.W. Pelham. 1988. "Of Thoughts Unspoken: Social Inference and the Self-Regulation of Behavior." *Journal of Personality and Social Psychology* 55, no. 5, p. 685.

[25]   Gailliot, M.T., R.F. Baumeister, C. Nathan DeWall, J.K. Maner, E.A. Plant, D.M. Tice, L.E. Brewer, and B.J. Schmeichel. 2007. "Self-Control Relies on Glucose as a Limited Energy Source: Willpower is More than a Metaphor." *Journal of Personality and Social Psychology* 92, no. 2, p. 325.

words on a screen as they evaluated the emotions of a person in a video, while another group simply watched the video. Sure enough, the group actively avoiding reading the words exhibited significantly lower glucose levels than their more passive counterparts.

Decision fatigue is not limited to humans as it turns out. In a memorable canine study, trained dogs were required to exert self-control to avoid distractions as they followed a command to stay in place for 10 minutes.[26] A comparison group of dogs simply stayed inside a dog crate for 10 minutes, an act requiring no particular mental exertion. After the time elapsed, the researchers presented both groups of dogs with a transparent dog toy containing tantalizing, but unreachable food. The dogs that focused on prolonged sitting abandoned their efforts to obtain the visible food more quickly than the crated group. Interestingly, when the actively sitting dogs were given a high glucose drink, they worked just as hard on the food puzzle as the well-rested crate group. Even dogs seem to suffer some level of fatigue after mental effort and can be replenished with glucose!

Relevance: When you actively work on your investment portfolio, you are consuming glucose and taxing your brain. This has implications for your subsequent energy levels and willpower. The more decisions you make, the more you will wear down your resolve. This may lead you to make more impulsive and less-optimal decisions late in the day, or after a particularly exhausting bout of work.

Processing Level: Decision fatigue acts on an intuition level. Our brains need resources in the form of rest and glucose in order to maintain control, delay immediate gratification, and move us into the reason level.

Brain Mechanisms: Decision fatigue occurs because our brains are depleted of fuel in the form of glucose. This seems to incur the most cost to us in the form of lowered levels of focus and resolve. The act of making financial decisions involves overcoming immediate rewards in order to gain more money down the road based on adherence to a narrative. We can consume more mental resources when we have to alter our thesis, or when

---

[26]   Miller, H.C. 2013. "The Effects of Initial Self-Control Exertion and Subsequent Glucose Consumption on Search Accuracy by Dogs." *Revista Argentina de Ciencias del Comportamiento (RACC)* 5, no. 2, p. 2.

we have to adjust based on structural events within an industry. When we exert mental control and actively work on a portfolio, we run the risk of decision fatigue as we accomplish more work.

Brain researchers at Dartmouth College scanned the brains of people on diets as they viewed pictures of foods.[27] The participants were next asked to actively suppress laughter while watching a comedy video. After the mental energy depletion of the laughter suppression, these dieters showed greater brain activity within a region of the basal ganglia that is tuned toward processing rewards and less activation within the amygdala, a region responsive to emotion (refer to Chapter 2). These results suggest that mental depletion, as observed in decision fatigue, leads us to be more responsive to immediate rewards and reduces our self-control. When the dieters received a dose of glucose the activity of their amygdala and basal ganglia returned to the pre-depleted state. Glucose is a key component in refreshing our brain's ability to maintain control over our decisions.

Who's vulnerable? All investors can fall victim to decision fatigue. This is particularly likely to impact active investors who monitor their positions regularly. Anyone who has spent many hours doing active research on a company should step back, take breaks, and stay fed and hydrated to avoid compromised decision making due to mental resource depletion.

Remedies:

- Remember that intuitive answers are not a true reflection of reality. Rather, they are a fit to your current cognitive state. If you are over-extended, then avoid making impulsive decisions. Remember to make the effort to accomplish higher quality analysis only after getting some rest.
- Reduce the number of overall decisions you make by implementing a defined process for decisions.
- Get sleep and adequate nutrition.
- Limit acting impulsively. Plot decisions in advance and track their numbers.

---

[27] Baumeister, R.F., and J. Tierney. 2012. *Willpower: Rediscovering the Greatest Human Strength*. Penguin.

- Avoid executing decisions at the same time you make them. Execute after trading hours.

The first virtue in a soldier is endurance of fatigue; courage is only the second virtue.

—Napoleon Bonaparte

PART II

CHAPTER 4

Our Memory Systems

Memory and the Brain

Memories form a core part of all of our experiences. What do you think of when you read the word "dog"? At the mere mention of the word, we've just primed you to think dog-related thoughts. Images of dogs may spontaneously pop into mind. You may think about your own dogs, a common breed, or perhaps the Taco Bell Chihuahua. If we were in a memory lab, we could reliably demonstrate that you would now be faster to produce dog-associated words such as "cat," "bone," and "collar." All of these associations leap to mind at the mere introduction of the term. In other words, we are biased toward certain thoughts based on our past experiences.

There are both voluntary and involuntary components to memory. Sometimes we will ourselves to actively recall details from the past. At other times, we find ourselves helplessly ruminating about a negative situation, or the features of our surroundings cause long-established associations to unwittingly enter our minds. The voluntary and involuntary parts of memory allow us some degree of control, but also leave us open to be guided by involuntary associations, or biases.

Our brains are not like audio or video recorders that capture a literal representation of our experiences. Rather, we store the *gist* of a situation, which is made up of the personally salient features of our experience. What is salient at any given time is determined both by the environment and by our preconceived expectations, or our mental models. Gist representations are rich in personal meaning, but impoverished in many literal details that were there for us to notice, but that somehow failed to capture our attention in the moment. Storing gist-based experiences distorts our mental models and investment narratives. We simply cannot create literal models of reality stored in full detail, as our attention and memory processes do not permit it. Out of the gate, our memories are biased toward presenting us with only the details we found relevant at the time we experienced them. As an added challenge, our current context can further bias us toward recalling certain things over others.

Distortions of Our Past

Take a moment to think about your first day of high school. What can you recall about that day? Some things may be literal memories. Perhaps you can think of a favorite shirt you wore, or the doors of the school entrance. Maybe you recall a teacher or two whom you particularly disliked. There may also be memories that feel more like non-specific impressions. You may recall vague flashes of the tumultuous mass of students moving about the hallways between classes, the yellow-tinted gleam of a polished gym floor with the rubberized smells, squeaks, and impacts of soles and dodge balls pounding off of bleachers, padded walls, and fellow students. You may recall feeling a general sense of anxiety about navigating a new building, surviving the new social scene, and coping with hopelessly tall, confident upper-classmen out to hassle you.

These types of experiences are all part of human memory. Some things we get right. We have accurate recall for many of the ground truth facts. You probably remember the features of the building relatively well. Some things we get wrong. If you ever visited your high school as an adult you probably found the whole experience much less dramatic. Without your peers present and your adolescent perspective, the place just isn't the same. Even if you do not recall all of your teachers, you would likely be able to recognize them if you were to leaf through an old yearbook.

Krawczyk attended his 20th high school reunion some years back after having lived a couple of decades in other parts of the country. One of the games played at this reunion involved attempting to recall as many high school teachers as possible. He gave up on the effort after a disappointing output of 10 or so names. After years of disuse, the names and faces had faded; however, a glance at the old yearbook enabled a remarkable renewal of these memories. The memories were there, but had simply become less accessible.

Personal memories are highly biased and may even be unique to us. Researchers call these *autobiographical* memories. They are typically less fact-based than recalling specific people and names. They are more like impressions intertwined with our personal feelings at the time of the experience. These memories are highly plastic. They flex and morph over the years becoming intertwined with our sense of self—who we were then fused with who we grew up to be. Our own perspective becomes bound up within these memories, as we are their authors. These are the memories that make eyewitness testimony unreliable and lead to heartfelt disagreements among siblings about who did what to whom years ago.

Misconceptions play a prominent role in my view of the world.
—George Soros

Altered States in Memory

Punk rock musicians, Greg Graffin and Brett Gurewitz of the band *Bad Religion,* frequently compose songs about scientific topics. In their song *Shattered Faith*, the protagonist is described as being an "imperfect moral meaning extractor." This phrase insightfully summarizes our memory systems. We store an incomplete, or distorted, version of reality that has been tinted by our emotional states and infused with personal meanings generated within our brains. Our memories are made up of ground truth facts mixed with the associations and emotions that our brains read into those data. In the words of Graffin and Gurewitz, "the method is the simple synthesis of the past and present state"—the past, as evoked from memory mixed with our interpretations of the present state of the world.

In Chapter 2, we discussed the work of brain physiologist, Joaquin Fuster, who described the brain as performing a *perception-action cycle.*[1] According to Fuster, we take information into memory from our perceptual systems, primarily housed in areas at the back and sides of the brain. We then build an impression, or mental model of the world that becomes imprinted with our own associations. We can use these mental models to formulate plans and take action. We influence our situation and then receive feedback with which to update our mental representations. All of this takes place in a rapid and fluid way (refer to Figure 4.1).

---

[1]   Fuster, J. 2015. *The Prefrontal Cortex.* Academic Press.

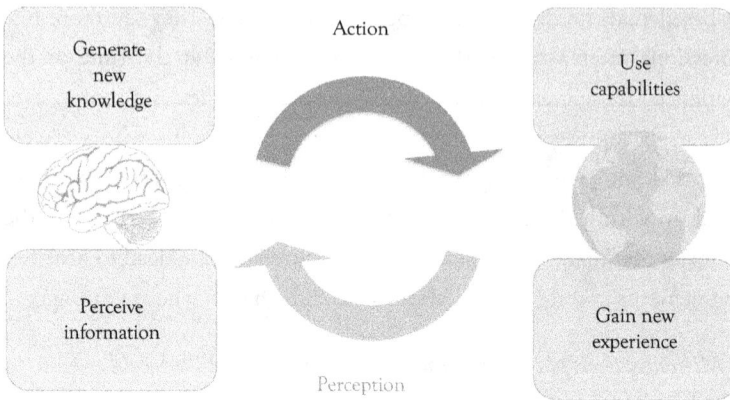

Figure 4.1 The perception-action cycle.

Figure based on Fuster, J.M. 2011. "Hayek in Today's Cognitive Neuroscience." *In Hayek in Mind: Hayek's Philosophical Psychology*, pp. 3–11. Emerald Group Publishing Limited.

Memory is active, dynamic, and personal. We can bring to mind past events at will. We can actively suppress thinking about particular memories. There are also times when we find ourselves ruminating, as we try unsuccessfully to avoid thinking about a particular situation. Memories do not merely appear for our examination and then return unchanged to the depths of our knowledge base. Rather, our brains perform active work on our memories and when we shelve them back into the recesses of our non-conscious mind, they are not the same. When we next recall the memory, it will emerge in an altered state, modified by the incorporation of any new thoughts that we had applied to it during our last round of examination. This dynamic process allows memories to reshape over time and with repeated examination. We can embellish our personal memory of a situation by talking to others, or by reading news about an event.

Famous events such as the Kennedy assassination and September 11 are also subject to modification by our memory systems, despite their initial dramatic quality.[2] Studies of famous event memories have

---

[2] Hirst, W., E.A., Phelps, R.L., Buckner, A.E. Budson, A. Cuc, J.D. Gabrieli, . . . and R. Meksin. 2009. "Long-Term Memory for the Terrorist Attack of September 11: Flashbulb Memories, Event Memories, and the Factors that Influence their Retention." *Journal of Experimental Psychology: General* 138, no. 2, p. 161.

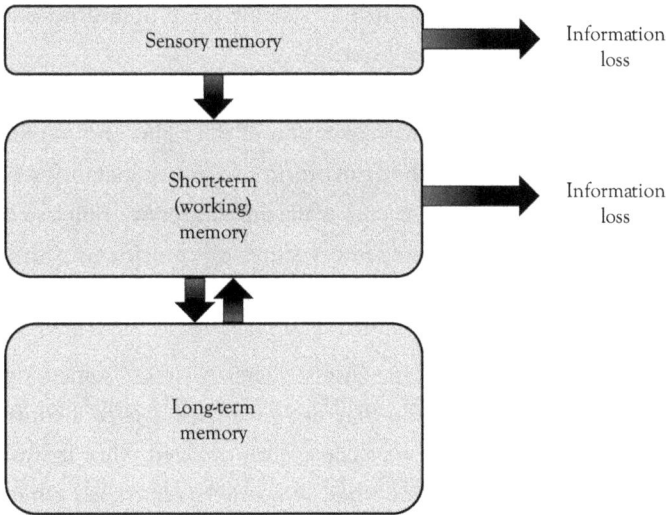

Figure 4.2 The Atkinson-Shiffrin model of memory

Source: Adapted from Atkinson, Richard C., and Richard M. Shiffrin. "Human Memory: A Proposed System and Its Control Processes." In *Psychology of Learning and Motivation*, vol. 2, pp. 89–195. Academic Press, 1968

reported that people lose some details and add others, making our mental representation an imperfect copy of the original over time. This distortion and modification process results in some critical biases that influence investment behavior.

Multiple Memory Systems

Researchers have not thought about memory as a single faculty for many years. Rather, there has been a sustained effort to characterize multiple memory systems. We need to be able to identify these different systems in order to understand and take steps to minimize memory-related cognitive biases.

Richard Atkinson and Richard Shiffrin developed one of the most influential models of memory.[3] Their model specified three interconnected stores, each having different characteristics (refer to Figure 4.2).

---

[3] Atkinson, R.C., and R.M. Shiffrin. 1968. "Human Memory: A Proposed System and Its Control Processes." In *Psychology of Learning and Motivation*, Vol. 2, pp. 89–195. Academic Press.

Decades later this model remains a helpful starting point in understanding the organization of our memory systems.

Atkinson and Shiffrin called our initial storage site *sensory memory*, which is a very short-lived trace representation of the sights and sounds that we have just experienced. The visual form of sensory memory was thought to last only fractions of a second, while the auditory version lasted perhaps a couple of seconds. These sensory stores can provide us with a slight reminder of what has just occurred, subtly shaping our intake of information.

You've probably experienced a sensory memory when something flashed in front of your vision. You may not have been able to identify it initially, but after a moment, you consciously realized what it was. Alternatively, you may recall a time when someone has muttered something and just as you are about to ask her to repeat herself, it dawns on you what she said. The sensory store is all about taking in new information. Despite the fleeting nature of these sensory representations, they can potentially bias us to attend to some information over others. Some of our instinctual and intuitive biases are influenced by these subtle sensory memories. Most of the sensory information is lost, as it is quickly overwritten by new incoming information, but when something grabs our attention its sensory trace moves through to the next storage bin called *short-term memory*.

You can think of Atkinson and Shiffrin's short-term store as representing your conscious mind. This information lasts approximately 10 seconds, unless you actively rehearse it. When you learn a new phone number, or Wi-Fi password, you will sometimes have to actively rehearse the digits before inputting them into your device. Rehearsal allows these temporary memories to remain alive within the short-term store.

Scientists now refer to the short-term store as *working memory*, as this updated term captures the fact that we perform active mental work on these representations.[4] Working memory acts as a mental stage for acting out our current thoughts. As with sensory memory, this store handles

---

[4] Baddeley, A. 2003. "Working Memory: Looking Back and Looking Forward." *Nature Reviews Neuroscience* 4, no. 10, p. 829.

both visual and auditory inputs on a temporary basis. The contents of working memory can be lost, or overwritten by interference from other information. If we lose focus before we input a phone number, then it is gone, lost from our consciousness. We'll have to ask for it again in those cases, as working memory is unforgiving. If we rehearse these memories enough, we can encode their contents into a more permanent store called *long-term memory.*

Long-term memory is the granddaddy of the memory stores. With massive capacity, this store holds all of the permanent memories accrued over your life. These may be experiences from last week, or events from early childhood. This is what most of us refer to as simply as "memory" in our daily lives. Information can move from long-term storage back into working memory. If you are asked to think about your favorite movie, you can quickly move long-term representations back into your conscious working memory. These can then be examined and reorganized, as we have mentioned earlier in this chapter.

Long-term memory is like your computer's hard drive, or your cloud account, while working memory is equivalent to your computer screen after you have opened a file from long-term memory. Just as you revise a blog entry, or modify a photo, when you perform active work upon the contents of your working memory, this sends a modified version of the representation back into your long-term store . This explains our ability to update our memories as we learn new facts that embellish, or alter them.

The arrows in the Atkinson Shiffrin memory model (Figure 4.2) illustrate that memory is dynamic. We can actively shift the contents around and perform work upon the representations. This active component to memory allows us to build mental models of investment positions. Those mental models can be updated and influenced by ongoing activity, provided we pay attention to it.

Mental models also influence our attention by subtly biasing us toward information that is consistent with our thesis and steering us away from the inconsistent information. Biased memories drop our recollection accuracy and cause us to limit our attention toward available information. These phenomena are consistent with our experiences and with neuroscience research about brain networks that are active during memory tasks. While long-term memory representations are stored in a variety of areas, short-term, or working memory representations depend upon the task network that we discussed in Chapter 2. This active representation network is aided by the default mode network for times when we place previous knowledge back into circulation in working memory.

Memory strength also depends upon how we *encode* new information and how we *retrieve* prior information. Both of these processes are essential to understanding how we think about our experiences.

Making Memories

The brain basis for memory is not as simple as the Atkinson Shiffrin model would suggest. That model was essentially a set of boxes containing a lifetime of memories. In actuality, our brains electrically merge content and context together into active networks. These networks provide the essence of memory storage and function.

The *hippocampus* is a critical brain structure that guides memory storage via brain networks. We have hippocampi on both sides of the brain buried within our temporal lobes. The term hippocampus is Latin for "seahorse," owing to its serpentine shape. It has an intricate anatomy composed of several distinct sub-areas. The 2014 Nobel Prize recipient, John O'Keefe, was one of the first researchers to discover that the hippocampus contains neurons that activate in response to navigational spatial patterns, somewhat like a GPS for tracking where we are in space. Later research would demonstrate that hippocampal neurons also respond to visual landmarks and to much of the verbal information that people take in, integrating this information together to form more permanent representations.

The critical value of the hippocampus for memory formation was dramatically illustrated by the case of Henry Molaison, who was simply known as "H.M." within the memory research community until his death in 2008.[5] Molaison suffered from epileptic fits, so neurosurgeons removed both of his hippocampi to limit his seizures. While the surgery

[5]   Squire, L.R. 2009. "The Legacy of Patient HM for Neuroscience." *Neuron* 61, no. 1, pp. 6–9.

was successful in diminishing seizure activity, it came with a devastating side effect. From the immediate aftermath of his surgery at age 27 through the remaining 55 years of his life, he was never able to form new memories normally. Molaison could attend to a situation for brief periods of time, provided it continued to engage his attention and working memory. Once he was distracted, or a few minutes had elapsed, the experience simply evaporated for him. Amazingly, Molaison could accurately describe the events that had occurred earlier in his life. Those memories had mysteriously remained after the surgery, suggesting that his early memories were different and stored elsewhere in the brain.

The story of Henry Molaison illustrates some key points about memory. First, the hippocampus is necessary to transfer information from working memory (that which we are actively attending to) into longer-term storage. Second, after a period of time, long-term memories no longer depend upon the hippocampus, as Molaison could recall his early autobiographical memories from before the surgery. Lastly, the hippocampus is involved in encoding new information into long-term memory, but is not essential for retrieving that information.

Researchers now describe the hippocampus as having a *time-limited* role in memory formation. Brain research studies in animals have demonstrated that memories remain if the hippocampus is removed weeks after an experience has occurred, but that they can be wiped clean if the hippocampi are removed just after an experience has occurred.[6] The details of hippocampal processing in humans may be more complex, as our rich emotions and consciousness also determine whether our experiences will be properly encoded and available for later recall.

So, *where is long-term memory* if not in the hippocampus? This remains an intriguing question in the research community. We don't know the answer for sure, but it appears that the neurons in the hippocampus represent memories as patterns of activity. Over time, these patterns eventually become encoded into the general network structure of the brain's cortex.

---

[6] Kim, J.J., and M.S. Fanselow. 1992. "Modality-Specific Retrograde Amnesia of Fear." *Science* 256, no. 5057, pp. 675–677.

For example, if a memory involves the sights and smells of the ocean, it is likely to involve some of the perceptual areas related to these experiences. Likewise, if you have a memory for a particular song, it will likely be stored in a network associated with your auditory cortex. Again, these are not high fidelity recordings of our experiences, but rather some essential features of our experience that we attended to and that became subsequently linked with our previous experiences. Evidence suggests that the hippocampus is highly active when we sleep and that it activates neural patterns that reflect the experiences of our previous day. This lends scientific support to the idea that we should defer a decision until tomorrow and take time to "sleep on it."

Older memories become hardened into the networks of our brains over time. These representations form our general tendencies when we encounter situations similar to those we have seen before. These older memories can then shape our behavior and the way we view the circumstances. In other words these long-term memories form the basis of many of our common behavioral biases.

Time moves in one direction, memory in another.
—William Gibson

What Is Memorable?

Our memory-biases are driven by two kinds of memories: interesting information and information that we think deeply about. Both situations can lead our brains to weight the information more heavily and may lead us to systematically distort our mental models in favor of that information.

Visualization

We have especially good memory for information that can be visualized. This is perhaps why pricing graphs are so compelling. Scientific studies are taken to be more credible if they include vivid brain images in addition to other measures of behavior.[7] Within finance, this may mean

---

[7] McCabe, D.P., and A.D. Castel. 2008. "Seeing is Believing: The Effect of Brain Images on Judgments of Scientific Reasoning." *Cognition* 107, no. 1, pp. 343–352.

that we over-fixate on graphs depicting moment-to-moment price movements. We may pay particular attention when research on a company includes comparisons to previous similar situations. The comparisons are memorable because we can imagine how things will play out, because we have seen something similar before.

Psychological researcher Alan Paivio provided a simple reason for the memorability of information that can be visualized.[8] He noted that words matter for later memory and we can always verbalize any situation. In cases in which we have a visual representation as well, we gain access to a second set of perceptual cues for triggering that information later in memory. In other words, the visual and verbal cues provide a richer representation that comes to mind more quickly.

Recency

Recent events weigh more heavily in our minds than older information. In the context of investing, many things change about a company and its price over time. The recent information can hijack our attention and distort our overall thesis. This common tendency is known as the *recency bias*, which we will cover in Chapter 5.

The hippocampus is important for representing recent information due to its time-limited role in memory. New information immediately depends upon the hippocampus, but not forever. Memories transition through a process called *consolidation*—a period when memories are being actively hard-coded into our cortical networks. Memories undergoing consolidation can bias out thinking, perhaps because our brains are actively working on their details. If we fixate too much on recent information, we can distort our mental models of a company toward over-weighting what has just happened.

Memory is deceptive because it is colored by today's events.

—Albert Einstein

---

[8] Paivio, A. 1990. *Mental Representations: A Dual Coding Approach*, vol. 9. Oxford University Press.

Emotion

Emotional situations are highly memorable. This makes potentially important information sneak past us and receive too little weight at times. At other times, we inappropriately overemphasize the impact of emotional information. Our amygdala and orbitofrontal cortex become highly activated by emotional situations making them engaging. These areas are also involved in generating arousal, which can add more richness to these memories.

Emotion is important for investing and you should treat emotional information as a highly salient cue. If we find a situation to be frightening, others will too. In addition to fear-inducing threats of losing money, it is also important to hold emotions in check to focus on long-range quantitative data that may be more illustrative of the future expected value of a company. In other words, take advantage of the natural edge afforded to emotional information, but don't neglect other information at its expense.

> *Cognitive psychology tells us that the unaided human mind is vulnerable to many fallacies and illusions because of its reliance on its memory for vivid anecdotes rather than systematic statistics.*
>
> —Steven Pinker

Deep Processing

Perhaps the most memorable information is that which we reflect upon deliberately. Actively investing our attention and working memory resources makes information memorable later on. Research has shown that stronger memories form when people actively consider the meaning of information including the associated sights, sounds, and smells of a situation. If you want to remember it later, then take the time to process it beyond its' surface characteristics. In other words, what you deliberately attend to integrates with your existing knowledge and tends to stick.

The memorability of deeply processed information illustrates some important truths about memory. When we spend a lot of time researching a position and make detailed forecasts, we are in the process of forging strong memories. This can lead to inappropriate levels of bias toward information that confirms our predictions (the *confirmation bias* discussed in Chapter 7). This over-weighted forecast may also become difficult to give up on, even when we should (this tendency leads to the *sunk-cost effect* also covered in Chapter 7).

> *Nothing is more responsible for the good old days than a bad memory.*
> —Franklin Pierce Adams

Retrieval

If you've gone to the trouble of doing careful research, how do you make sure you can remember the key facts at the appropriate time? This is the challenge of memory retrieval. There is often a natural alignment between quality encoding and a high probability of later retrieval, but these still remain separate processes. Even rich and deeply processed information may be unavailable at a later time simply because the *context* is so critical to guiding retrieval. You've heard this before if you have already read Chapter 2—context is key. Context drives our attention toward certain information, but it also triggers memories at particular moments. Without the right context, we are unlikely to gain an informational advantage because we cannot call all relevant memories to mind when they are most needed.

The Importance of Cues

Context guides us with *cues* to retrieve memory. A cue can be a sight, sound, or smell that triggers a particular memory. Cues vary in strength depending on how well they match the relevant memory. Scent is a very potent memory cue, as the hippocampal and emotional circuitry of the brain are closely associated with our olfactory brain areas. The scent of a particular perfume, or of a particular food can flood your mind with involuntary associations, even years after your original experiences. Cues can also be weakly relevant. If you've ever experienced a vague feeling of *déjà vu*, this may be related to the presence of weak memory cues. Sometimes cues partially activate a memory, but do not enable us to isolate the source of that memory. This may make the situation feel eerily familiar.

The overlap of cues heavily governs our memory retrieval. The presence of more cues from the original experience re-occurring in a retrieval context, ups the chances of retrieving the original memory. Researcher Alan Baddeley and his colleagues colorfully demonstrated this principle.[9] They asked a group of people to suit up in scuba gear and to remember a set of words presented to them while they were underwater. Another group simply tried to remember a series of words presented on land. Half of the people in each group later switched context, so that some people who learned underwater were tested about their memory for the words on land and vice versa. Others within each group were tested in the same environment in which they originally learned the words. People who recalled in the same place that they had learned showed the best overall memory. Being in the same context encouraged better memory retrieval, which included cues being reinstated by the similar setting. Perhaps it was the sight of bubbles, or the feeling of sluggish underwater movement that cued the words to enable superior memory performance if you had also witnessed these cues during study.

Memory retrieval has some down sides during investing. Some situations are highly similar to other investment positions you have held in the past. The similarities can evoke cues from your past positions and lead directly to biases based on re-invoking what you have done previously. There will inevitably be times when a situation looks similar to something you've seen before. This can be tricky, as the presence of cues can fool you into seeing similarities that just aren't there in the new position. Again, the context of the investing narrative is important in determining the types of information that come to mind.

Sleep

Mounting evidence indicates that sleep is intimately tied to our memory systems. While the precise functions of sleep remain somewhat mysterious, many researchers now believe that memories are consolidated during certain stages of our sleep cycle.

---

[9] Godden, D.R., and A.D. Baddeley. 1975. "Context-Dependent Memory in Two Natural Environments: On Land and Underwater." *British Journal of Psychology* 66, no. 3, pp. 325–331.

Bruce McNaughton and his colleagues described a fascinating sleep-memory study that illustrates this point.[10] They rigged up lab rats with head mounted electrode setups. These headsets could record from neurons within the rodents' hippocampus as the rats ran about navigating. McNaughton and his colleagues then analyzed the activity patterns from the location-sensitive neurons within the rat's brains. The electrode setups could also record from these same neurons later on when the rats slept. Remarkably, as the rodents slept their hippocampal neurons activated to reproduce the same location patterns that the rats had actually experienced earlier in the day. In other words, if you made three left turns and a right turn in order to get some cheese, your hippocampus reproduced that same spatial pattern later at night while you slept.

Does this mean the rats were enjoying thrilling dreams about navigating cheese mazes during the night? Could this mean that nightly your brain re-experiences your commute to your child's school, or a new restaurant?

We don't yet know how this sleep-state reproduction of the electrical patterns in our daily lives influences our experiences, but it appears likely that this activity during sleep has a lot to do with the hippocampal role in memory consolidation. After even a few hours of sleep, we will better remember the previous day, then if we choose to pull the infamous college "all-nighter." All-nighters rob our brains of their natural opportunity to solidify our memories enhancing their availability the next day. Lack of sleep also deprives our brains of the down time that has a restorative effect on our attention and memory systems. We make worse decisions on little sleep and this can negatively affect investment performance along with a host of other daily activities. Try to avoid making snap investment decisions on too little sleep.

Distortions of Memory

Memories are highly plastic and are constantly being modified. Mounting evidence points to changes in neural networks as the basis for memories.

---

[10]   Wilson, M.A., and B.L. McNaughton. 1994. "Reactivation of Hippocampal Ensemble Memories During Sleep." *Science* 265, no. 5172, pp. 676–679.

These changes occur by points of communication between neurons changing in their biochemical properties. A common phrase for neuroscience students is that neurons that "fire together, wire together." In other words, when a contact point between neurons within a network is excited repeatedly, then that same contact point will be strengthened. Much like weight training enhances the strength of your muscles and running strengthens your cardiovascular system.

The elastic properties of memory in the brain are an extension of what we have already discussed regarding attention in Chapter 2. We are quick to notice and attend to certain details to the exclusion of others. Likewise, we grab onto particular salient features of a memory and gradually lose other features. Ultimately, this means that we often store the gist of a situation rather than the veridical details. Gist representations leave us open to bias, as our brains wipe away details in favor of storing a more parsimonious *general picture* of a situation.

People's loss of detail from memory results in eyewitness testimony being dicey in a courtroom. When two witnesses are convinced that they saw different people committing a crime, we are tempted to think that one is lying. Such a situation may arise because one (or both) of their memories has become distorted over time, altered by selectively erasing details leaving only some parts of the prior situation. Salient, obvious features such as glasses, a hat, a hoodie, or a persons' ethnicity can remain strong, while details such as specific facial features, height, and hair color can be lost. The results can be disastrous, as many people have been exonerated after years of wrongful imprisonment based on later DNA evidence. In many cases, eyewitness testimony was one of the key lines of evidence that led to a guilty verdict in the first place.[11] When we store the gist of any situation we risk eliminating important information simply because it didn't fit our personal version of what was going on. Our gist memories are open to further corruption by the insertion of false additional details that bolster the clarity of our particular "gist version" of events. The result can be a faulty memory that we are confident in—an insidious mix for

---

[11]   Baraybar, J.P. 2008. "When DNA is not Available, Can We Still Identify People? Recommendations for Best Practice." *Journal of Forensic Sciences* 53, no. 3, pp. 533–540.

predicting the future of your investments. Processes need to be built in, so that you are not overly influenced by gist memories.

Building memories is a mixed bag. We need memory in order to do our work. Knowing what has happened in the past is often a critical guide toward what will happen in the future. There are however, times when our memories become distorted and this can lead us astray in our further analysis.

No man has a good enough memory to be a successful liar.

—Abraham Lincoln

Memory Biases Preview

In the next chapter, we will discuss a series of cognitive biases that are based on our memory systems. You can make sense of many of these biases and see why they occur using what we've just covered in this chapter.

Our memory systems are limited in capacity. Only some memories make it through our sensory storage systems to working memory. Only some items in working memory survive transfer to long-term storage. Our long term memories can shift over time as we learn more. Critically, we cannot completely determine what makes it into long-term memory much of the time. This is why we must actively research so that we are not left having to trust someone else's opinion. Accurate memories occur when we play an active role in mastering new information and working to organize it appropriately.

Distortions arise from the properties of our memory systems. We helplessly attend to emotional information over bland information. Our brains naturally prioritize recent information over older information. We also tend to recall things that we recognized first about a position, even when that information proves to be less relevant or even inaccurate. Our history with a position can also lead us to become overly attached and force us to lose objectivity.

To avoid these mental traps, it is necessary to revisit one's narrative often. Keeping your original impressions close at hand can help to guard against key details slipping away and inadvertent drift toward misremembering things as being different than they appeared earlier. It can also help to strategically update your thinking on a position by talking your thesis through with a colleague. We will discuss specific methods that you can put into practice to reduce memory biases and revisit these techniques in Chapter 8.

Instinct, Intuition, and Reason

In Chapter 2 we discussed the role of thinking in generating cognitive biases. *Instinct, intuition, reason* are all relevant in how we monitor and make use of our memories. *Metacognition* is the term that researchers use to describe our knowledge about the state of our memories. In other words, metacognition is how we think about our thinking. Trouble-somely, we have little access to the inner workings of our memory systems. Distorted memories can still feel quite real to us. We sometimes lose details without realizing it and insert new details that are from a similar, but separate situation. There are also times when there is only a weak relationship between confidence in our memories and their accuracy.

A distorted memory can feel just as real as the day the situation was observed. We may recall the authoritative voice of news anchor Peter Jennings discussing the dire implications of the collapse of Lehman Brothers. This would be a false memory, but a believable one (Peter Jennings actually had passed away in 2005). There may be times when you have repeatedly heard a particular fish tale that keeps getting more elaborate over time. This stretching of the truth may be due to a gradual drift that occurs to many memories that are only occasionally recalled. As we move further from the actual occurrence of a situation, the previous bending of the truth becomes a jumping-off point for the next retelling and so on until the memory no longer resembles what it had once been.

Summary

- Building memories involves filtering reality into a set of features that we consider relevant, then storing only those relevant features.
- Our memory systems can be thought of in terms of immediate sensory storage, active information that we can work on,

and long-term memories that remain with us, but are hidden from examination until we focus on them.

- The hippocampus is a brain area important for memory storage. This brain region is found on both sides of our temporal lobes and is necessary for a limited time in transferring our stored memories.
- Memory involves active encoding to provide a solid trace for later retrieval.
- Visualization affects our memories. Information that has a visual representation is more memorable to us.
- Recently experienced situations are more memorable than older ones.
- Emotional situations lead to exceptionally strong memories. This can be troublesome, as our emotions are personal and can distort our memories toward storing only some details, while leaving out other important details.
- Deeply processed information tends to stick with us. This includes information that we have built into a narrative and information that we actively relate to our previous memories.
- Retrieval is influenced by the context of a situation. When a current context has more overlap with the previous context in which we encountered information, it will cue more memories from the past.
- Sleep facilitates building memories and may have an active role in creating higher fidelity traces in our neural networks.
- Memories are modified constantly as we update based on new information, fail to retrieve some details, and unwittingly add in other new details that did not happen.
- Exposure to new information that is similar to our prior experiences can change memories.
- Revisiting one's narrative often and updating by talking it through may be effective in reducing biases toward limited feature sets/information sets in investing.

Just as food eaten without appetite is a tedious nourishment, so does study without zeal damage the memory by not assimilating what it absorbs.
—Leonardo da Vinci

Recommended Readings

Schacter, D.L. 2008. *Searching for Memory: The Brain, The Mind, and the Past.* Basic Books.

Atkinson, R.C., and R.M. Shiffrin. 1968. "Human Memory: A Proposed System and its Control Processes." In *Psychology of Learning and Motivation*, vol. 2, pp. 89–195. Academic Press, 1968.

CHAPTER 5

Memory Biases

Memory has a profound influence on our lives. As we discussed in Chapter 4, there are strong reasons that we remember some things and forget others. We also discussed the role of context in determining both what we encode into memory and what we retrieve later. Memory can influence us on a regular basis in investment analysis. We pick up on particular cues in the current context. These remind us of situations and dynamics that we have seen before. At the same time, we may become blind to important information that is simply less emotional, less obvious, or less familiar. This selective information processing captures some important behavioral biases. Some of these biases can be helpful, but they can also force us into committing critical errors when it comes to analyzing our positions.

Memories are dynamic and flexible. Their strength varies over time with newer information often being prioritized and more memorable at any given moment. Over time our memories drift, so that what we initially remembered becomes sketchy and less detailed. This leads us toward seeing a distorted version of reality when we consider the current state of a position. We tend to add in extra details that commonly occur. For example when a stock is dropping, we often add a variety of common reasons for losses into our assessment of the position, even when there is no direct evidence for those reasons. If we hold the stock, we may misremember some of these added inferential details as having actually occurred. The next thing you know, you may be basing your expectations on a very flawed set of presumptions.

In this chapter, we cover a variety of biases that are directly tied to our memory systems. Some have to do with our likelihood of later recall, while others are due to the undue influence of things we have seen before affecting our thinking about current positions.

*Right now I'm having amnesia and déjà vu at the same time. I think
I've forgotten this before.*

—Steven Wright

Availability Bias

Definition: We prioritize information that is readily available. The *availability bias* occurs when this highly accessible information has more
influence on our thinking than other equally relevant, but less accessible
information at the moment of need.

Background: The availability bias is one of Daniel Kahneman and
Amos Tversky's most influential cognitive heuristics (mental shortcuts).
In a landmark experiment from 1973, Tversky and Kahneman asked
people the following question:

*"suppose one samples a word (of three letters or more) at random from an
English text. Is it more likely that the word starts with "r" or that "r" is the
third letter?"*[1]

Take a moment to try this yourself. If you're like most people, you
guessed that more words start with "r," as you can quickly generate more
words that begin with an "r." In reality, there are many more words in
which "r" appears as the third letter. The high availability of words starting with "r" steers us astray when we attempt to answer this simple question. This is precisely the result reported by Kahneman and Tversky over
40 years ago. The availability bias can skew our estimates of probability
and distort the weights and values that we place on different investment
factors.

Relevance: Some information just pops into mind faster and is therefore given an oversized priority. A hyper-focus on available information
can lead to weak analysis.

Economists, Doron Kliger and Andrey Kudryavtsev, investigated the
effect of availability bias on investors' reactions to analyst recommendations. Kliger and Kudryavtsev considered daily market returns to be a

---

[1] Tversky, A., and D. Kahneman. 1973. "Availability: A Heuristic for Judging
Frequency and Probability." *Cognitive Psychology* 5, no. 2, pp. 207–232.

reliable source of highly available information.[2] They reported that positive price reactions to recommendation upgrades on individual securities were stronger when released on days when the market had positive market returns. Conversely, negative price reactions to recommendation downgrades were stronger when they were paired with negative returns. Furthermore, the magnitude of availability bias associated with market performance was negatively correlated with company market capitalization, and positively correlated with the stock's historical volatility.

Processing Level: Availability operates at the intuition level. Highly available memories *feel* like a sound reflection of reality, but they can be distorted and mislead us (just as in Tversky and Kahneman's "letter r" problem).

Brain Mechanisms: Availability bias arises from the brain's memory retrieval circuits. Numerous studies have identified the frontal lobes, hippocampus, and the default mode network areas as being active for memory retrieval.[3] Regrettably, the most quickly accessible memories are not always the most important and they may not even be relevant to properly assessing a situation. Some nodes and links within the widely distributed memory networks are stronger and these result in quicker access to information.

Ultimately, the frontal lobes may be the biggest cortical culprit in generating availability bias. The frontal lobes set the stage for a particular question or problem in investment analysis. They are also involved in assessing the fit between an answer from memory and our mental sketch of the problem. When the fit feels right, we stop our analysis prematurely, perhaps having placed too much focus on the readily accessible information.

Who's vulnerable? Availability is a widely observed human bias. All investors risk focusing too much on the most available information, as this stems from the core operations of our memory systems.

---

[2] Kliger, D., and A. Kudryavtsev. 2010. "The Availability Heuristic and Investors' Reaction to Company-Specific Events." *The Journal of Behavioral Finance* 11, no. 1, pp. 50–65.

[3] Rugg, M.D., and K.L. Vilberg. 2013. "Brain Networks Underlying Episodic Memory Retrieval." *Current Opinion in Neurobiology* 23, no. 2, pp. 255–260.

Remedies:

- Write down your early assumptions before performing research. You can revisit these initial assumptions over time to see how well evidence aligns with them. This exercise can help you to refresh your memory about your projected narrative and avoid inappropriately emphasizing only the most memorable information at the moment.

- You should keep track of instances that arise in your research process that could be affected by the availability of information. Take note of a variety of perspectives and a diversity of information in an investment journal. This will help you to examine the validity of your interpretations throughout the time that you hold a position.

- Remember that intuitive answers are not a true reflection of reality. Rather, they are a fit to your current mental sketch of the situation. Be vigilant about answers that feel intuitively correct. There may be other important information that we already know and this can be recalled with effort to accomplish higher quality analysis.

* also see *primacy effect* and *recency bias*

> *Your memory is a monster; you forget—it doesn't. It simply files things away. It keeps things for you, or hides things from you—and summons them to your recall with a will of its own. You think you have a memory; but it has you!*
>
> —John Irving

Primacy Effect

Definition: The *primacy effect* occurs when we experience an unusually high recall level for items that we encountered early in a set of information. For example, when learning a group of new people's names, you experience a primacy effect when you remember the first few people's names better than the rest.

Background: The primacy effect emerges as a core principle of our memory systems and forms part of the serial position curve in memory

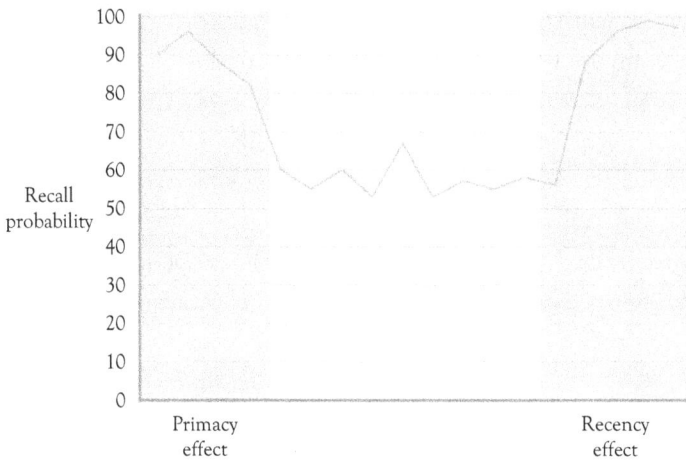

Figure 5.1 Serial-position curve plotting the probability of later recall based on the time that information is studied

(see Figure 5.1). In most learning situations both early and late information are prioritized. Primacy effects have been demonstrated in hundreds of list-learning studies, in which someone is asked to remember a sequence of unrelated words at a later time. Typically, the first three to four words will be more likely to be remembered later than other items in the list.[4] Why does this happen?

As more items build up over the course of a learning period they tend to muddle together losing their distinctiveness as competition increases for your limited memory space. Items presented earliest also afford us the most time to rehearse them.

Frank Yates and Shawn Curley demonstrated a primacy effect in contingency judgments, a case of reasoning under uncertainty.[5] They asked people to evaluate the potential relationship between color and location between fictional types of plants (in reality there was no relationship) (see Illusion of Control in Chapter 3). Participants showed a bias toward estimating higher relatedness between color and location if they had been

---

[4] Murdock, Jr, B.B. 1962. "The Serial Position Effect of Free Recall." *Journal of Experimental Psychology* 64, no. 5, p. 482.

[5] Yates, J.F., and Shawn, P.C. 1986. "Contingency Judgment: Primacy Effects and Attention Decrement." *Acta Psychological* 62, no. 3, pp. 293–302.

presented with early data suggesting such a relationship. Despite seeing more examples that did not support a relationship later on, the initial impression persisted skewing people's judgments. This result suggests that our initial impressions may have an undue influence related to the primacy effect. This also means that important information taken in later can be undervalued.

Relevance: The primacy effect can disrupt financial performance because it leads us to be biased toward information that we acquired early on. As you construct a narrative, you are actively shaping the memories associated with your position. This can lead to an undesirable situation in which you become particularly tied to your early ideas. This can lead to sticking with a bad narrative for too long, as new information requires extra weighting in order to overcome the outsized prioritization of the previously constructed narrative.

Processing Level: Primacy effects operate at the intuition level. We frequently have difficulty realizing that we are assigning unusually high weight to information learned early in the process of analyzing a company, it just feels like the right information.

Brain Mechanisms: The primacy effect comes about from both encoding and retrieval circuits within the brain. Like other memory biases this involves the frontal lobes, which enable us to match memories to the proper context. The hippocampus and other temporal lobe areas are relevant to prioritizing some memory information over others.

Who's vulnerable? Growth investors who hold a position for a long duration risk focusing too much on information learned early on in their analysis.

Remedies:

- Regularly review your position assumptions. This can help you to avoid prioritizing information learned early on in an analysis.
- Keep a journal to track the emergence of later information. This will enable you to re-calibrate the weight that you are placing on information throughout your research process.
- You should draft a simple one-page investment pre-mortem document after you conduct an analytical review (see Chapter 8). This document should state the premises of the assessment

and a short summary of the material data that support it. Reviewing this document as events unfold will help you to avoid over-emphasizing early ideas and initial information. This should allow you to gain a balanced perspective on information as events unfold.

* also see *availability bias* and *recency bias*

Life can only be understood backwards; but it must be lived forwards.
—Soren Kierkegaard

Recency Bias

Definition: Recency bias occurs when we prioritize recently learned information over older information. While it may be appropriate to alter course in accordance with breaking news about a company, or pricing changes in a stock, recency bias plagues investors when they elevate the importance of recent information above older information that is equally relevant.

Background: The recency bias is part of the classic serial position curve identified in the memory research field (see Figure 5.1). When memory researchers present a set of items to be remembered later, the final few items in the set tend to be remembered at a high level. These items have an advantage as they were presented recently with nothing following, so this information can remain active in working memory. Recency bias in finance also occurs when long-term memories that have been activated recently become highly available to us (which feeds the availability bias discussed earlier in this chapter). In this respect, recency bias relates most to the timing of the information.

Relevance: Recency bias occurs when investors become overly fixated on what has happened in the short run. This can be problematic for any situation, but may be especially troublesome for stocks held over a long period that have continued to rise for what looks like a sustained period of growth. The price may be more cyclical than recent history suggests and recency bias can blind us to important information that occurred earlier in time.

Processing Level: Recency bias is an intuition-based tendency. Our memory systems retrieve recently experienced situations more easily compared to older memories. We do not have much conscious control of this phenomenon.

Brain Mechanisms: Recency bias derives from the brain's working memory system. This system is associated with the *task network* described in Chapter 2 that includes the outer portions of the frontal and parietal lobes. This brain network actively maintains incoming information, which is vividly expressed in our stream of consciousness and therefore difficult to ignore compared to older information.

We may also experience recency bias due to highly accessible long-term memories that were recently encoded. Evidence suggests that these memories depend upon the hippocampus for their expression (see Chapter 4) and are therefore different, and possibly more accessible, than older memories that have been encoded into the broader brain networks. Older memories appear to need less hippocampal involvement to be retrieved.[6] Recent hippocampal-based memories may therefore have an undue influence on our investing performance owing to their privileged accessibility. This may lead us to inadvertently ignore prior information that is strongly relevant to our current analysis, but just less accessible at the moment because it is overshadowed by recent information.

Who's vulnerable? Short-term traders risk over-emphasizing what has happened very recently. Investors who pay too much attention to news sources also risk being overly influenced by recent information.

Remedies:

- Review your initial position assumptions, as this can help to avoid focusing too much on the most recent events that have unfolded. Take note of whether new information runs counter to your initial thesis. This can help you to avoid unwittingly altering your thinking on a position as new and potent information emerges.

---

[6] Zola-Morgan, S.M., and L.R. Squire. 1990. "The Primate Hippocampal Formation: Evidence for a Time-Limited Role in Memory Storage." *Science* 250, no. 4978, pp. 288–290.

- Keep a journal to remind yourself of information about the position that had occurred weeks-to-months earlier. This will help you to properly weight recent information and allow you to compare it to your earlier thoughts.
- Draft a one-page investment conclusion document after your analytical review (see Chapter 8). This document serves as a record of the initial premises for a position with a short summary of the data supporting it. Review this document throughout the time you hold a position to properly weight information and avoid over-emphasizing the most recent information.
- Document your analysis carefully and regularly revisit your thoughts on it.

* also see *availability bias* and *primacy effect*

what have you done for me lately ?

—Eddie Murphy

Endowment Effect

Definition: We experience the *endowment effect* when our preferences for things we own grow out of proportion relative to their objective value. Whenever we obtain something (an object, a job, a stock holding), we gain experience with it. This experience builds memories that we become attached to. Soon the memories lead us to prefer something that we own to something of equivalent (or higher) value that we do not currently own, even if it is not *objectively better* than the alternative.

Background: Economist, Jack Knetsch, colorfully illustrated the endowment effect in a gift exchange study.[7] He randomly gave people either a coffee mug, or a chocolate bar; two items of approximately equal value. The recipients next had an opportunity to exchange their gift for the alternative. Roughly half of the people should have been willing to make this

---

[7] Knetsch, J.L. 1989. "The Endowment Effect and Evidence of Nonreversible Indifference Curves." *American Economic Review* 79, no. 5, pp. 1277–1284.

exchange assuming no particular preference biases existed in the groups. In actuality, only about 10 percent of people agreed to exchange gifts! This result suggests that people express an illogical soft spot for something they already own relative to other possibilities, even when the item acquired is not particularly valuable and was only recently acquired.

In a related study, Knetsch, along with Daniel Kahneman and Richard Thaler, asked people to explicitly set prices for coffee mugs.[8] Some people received a mug and were asked to state the lowest price for which they would sell it. A second group was asked to set a price for which they would buy the mug. As in the prior study by Knetsch, if both groups acted rationally, they should have evaluated the price at roughly the same point. In contrast, sellers set the mug's value at almost twice that of the buyers!

Relevance: If you have been inclined to hold a position just a bit too long and ended up losing money by failing to give up on it, then you likely fell victim to the endowment effect. Things we already own gain value for two reasons. First, if you haven't lost money on a position, then it can appear less risky than unknown alternatives. Second, you build up a personal history owning a stock and the memories of your work become intertwined with it, artificially inflating its subjective value. This can inappropriately distort our sense of value for an owned stock over an equivalent, or even a superior position, that we do not yet own.

Processing Level: The endowment effect operates at both the instinct and intuition levels of our thinking. Often times our own experiences become embellished with an emotionally positive tone. It can become difficult to see beyond this rosy glow, as emotions have a highly automatic quality about them.

Brain Mechanisms: The endowment effect is related to our frontal lobes. The middle portion of the frontal lobes is active in generating subjective value and this area interacts with other brain areas including the amygdala, hippocampus, and other temporal lobe memory structures. When we have a wealth of memories (especially positive ones) related to owning

---

[8] Kahneman, D., J.L. Knetsch, and R.H. Thaler. 1991. "Anomalies: The Endowment Effect, Loss Aversion, and Status Quo Bias." *Journal of Economic Perspectives* 5, no. 1, pp. 193–206.

a particular stock, these memories enhance subjective value, sometimes too much. This can dangerously drive us to persist in believing that a troubled company will turn around, or that a high performing one will continue to rise indefinitely.

Who's vulnerable? Long-term investors who focus on long-range trends can often become very attached to positions that they have held for an extended period of time.

Remedies:

- Draft a simple one-page investment pre-mortem document after completing your analytical review. This document includes the premises of the assessment and summarizes the data that support it. This document should provide a road-map for the execution of the investment. You can also antici-pate actions that you can take toward potential developments *prior to* their occurrence. All of this is drafted before you have held the position and become psychologically attached to it.
- A stop-loss level is an effective means to overcome endow-ment effects. This will allow you to limit your losses after you have become attached to a position.
- Discipline yourself to carry out the stop-loss unless you have evidence for a near term catalyst that has yet to be realized and is unappreciated by the market.
- You should periodically review each position in your portfo-lio and ask yourself if you did not own a particular position today would you buy it at the current price and with the cur-rent position size. This is a way you can use framing to your advantage in combating bias.

No one can come and claim ownership of my work. I am the creator of it, and it lives within me.

—Prince

Consistency Bias

Definition: While we like to be consistently correct in our analysis, unfor-tunately we sometimes make mistakes. People perform some remarkable mental gymnastics in order to align facts to support a favored conclusion. This process of reasoning in reverse can cripple investment performance if you have become too attached to a narrative. Such conditions can encourage a *consistency bias,* in which we inappropriately over-weight information that aligns with a favored narrative and wish things to play out in accordance with our theories.

Background: Consistency bias was a cornerstone of social psychology in the mid-to-late 20th century. Psychologist, Leon Festinger, championed cognitive dissonance theory around this time.[9] Festinger was interested in how people dealt with behavior that contradicted their beliefs. Under such conditions, he predicted that people would experience *cognitive dissonance,* an uncomfortable feeling arising from the mismatch between behavior and beliefs. Festinger theorized that people respond by altering their beliefs to realign them with behavior to re-establish consistency.

In a memorable test of cognitive dissonance theory from 1974, Mark Zanna and Joel Cooper asked college students to write an essay arguing *for* a tuition increase, clearly an unpopular financial outcome and against their best interests.[10] Zanna and Cooper theorized that people would adjust their tuition-related attitudes after having argued in favor of the increase—a behavior highly discomforting to a poor college student. To test for the effect of discomfort, Zanna and Cooper cleverly gave people a placebo pill in the experiment. They told one group of participants that the pill would cause them to have a tense reaction. This group failed to report greater agreement with the tuition increase after writing the essay, as they could discount any essay-related discomfort to being a result of the (supposedly) anxiety-producing pill. The experimenters told a second group that the pill would have no effect. Consistent with the theory, the people in this group claimed to agree more with a tuition hike after they wrote the essay. In other words, they changed their viewpoint to support the essay writing in order to realign their behavior and actions.

---

[9]   Festinger, L. 1962. *A Theory of Cognitive Dissonance,* vol. 2. Stanford University Press.

[10]   Zanna, M.P., and J. Cooper. 1974. "Dissonance and the Pill: An Attribution Approach to Studying the Arousal Properties of Dissonance." *Journal of Personality and Social Psychology* 29, no. 5, p. 703.

People can move their opinions around in remarkable ways in order to achieve internal consistency. This powerful motive can lead us to make erroneous decisions in the quest to appear stable and reliable to both ourselves and others.

Relevance: Consistency bias plagues investors who begin with a strong idea on a position. The investor may tell others about their thesis, or worse yet, write about their position. Putting ideas on paper, or telling others, can over-commit us to taking a particular stance. If and when events and pricing do not play out in accordance with the initial narrative, the investor may double down on the original idea and hold the position too long out of obligation to preserve internal and external consistency.

Processing Level: Consistency bias is both an instinct and intuition bias. People possess a highly protective emotional instinct to appear consistent. Acting on this tendency is often intuitive, rather than carefully thought out.

Brain Mechanisms: The consistency bias is likely associated with the default mode network of the brain. This set of areas is active when we consider our internal state of mind. When conflict is experienced, a midline brain area called the anterior cingulate becomes activated. These areas likely interact with temporal lobe memory regions associated with storing information about a position and our previous beliefs about that narrative. Self-monitoring is necessary to notice and overcome this tendency toward consistency. Activation of the task-mode fronto-parietal networks is associated with this ability.[11]

Who's vulnerable? Investors who pitch an idea to a larger group tend to be the most susceptible to consistency bias. The failure to adjust due to consistency bias can be devastating to one's portfolio.

Remedies:

- Consider avoiding any advocacy outside of your investment group or team.
- If you do share an idea, try to emphasize the risks and assign them specific probabilities. You may want to acknowledge that it is a desirable bet, but that it may not yeild a desirable outcome if the risks come to fruition.

---

[11] McGuire, P.K., D.A. Silbersweig, and C.D. Frith. 1996. "Functional Neuroanatomy of Verbal Self-Monitoring." *Brain* 119, no. 3, pp. 907–917.

- It is important to clearly delineate the risks associated with various outcomes associated with any investment thesis. Having voiced alternative and unfavorable outcomes, you can avoid appearing inconsistent if you change your mind.
- It may help to state up front that your opinion is based on the facts as you currently see them, but also state the caveat that your opinion could change at any time if new information comes to light, or if the hand of fate tips to favor the risks in your assessment.

Progress is impossible without change, and those who cannot change their minds cannot change anything.

—George Bernard Shaw

Sunk Cost Effect

Definition: Have you ever held onto a position just a bit too long simply because you had paid a higher price and you wanted to recoup your loss before exiting? Perhaps you have had a position to which you devoted a significant amount of time and effort researching and you avoided exit because to do so would mean you had wasted all of your effort. In each instance, the decision to hold on may have been due to the *sunk cost effect,* a phenomenon in which we continue to pay for something, or persist in performing some action, simply because we have already invested a lot of time and money in it. This may occur because of a highly priced initial purchase of a position, or because you have spent a significant amount of time researching it. In either case you may be at risk of "throwing good money after bad" because you have already devoted a lot to the position.

Background: The sunk cost fallacy occurs regularly in political and corporate life. People do not like to appear to be wrong. When a politician has spent a lot on a public project, she may continue to spend even if the project is over budget and going poorly. Likewise, many companies stay with a bad idea too long, hoping things will turn around, all the while worrying that they will be seen as "flip-flopping" if they make a change. The choice to "stay the course" is not always made wisely. We tend to want to live up to our commitments and this can indeed hurt one's portfolio.

Hal Arkes and Catherine Blumer demonstrated the sunk cost effect in a memorable experiment at a theater.[12] They sold three groups of people season tickets; one group paid full price and the other two other groups received a discount. The researchers then monitored attendance at theater productions. One group showed significantly more attendance than the rest—those who had paid full price. Even though each group had committed money to the tickets, the amount that they had already committed made a difference. Since the discounts were distributed randomly, one would expect a roughly equal number of persistent hard core theatre goers to exist in all three groups. It appears that the sunk cost brought up the attendance level for those who had paid more initially.

Relevance: Sunk costs have wide-ranging effects on investing behavior. The sunk cost effect is often referred to as being a *fallacy*, as it is a case of illogical behavior. At any given moment, all of us can choose how to spend our resources in a way that gives us the most future benefit, regardless of how much we've already put into a particular course of action. It is critical that we not lose sight of this fact when investing. The market does not care how much you paid for the initial stock, or how much effort you have put into your research. Remember, only you value the time and effort that you have already lost on a declining position. This is because you have formed autobiographical memories that may inappropriately compel you to stay with an investment when it no longer makes objective sense to do so.

Processing Level: Sunk cost effects operate at both the instinct and intuition levels. It feels intuitively correct to stay with our commitments in many areas of our lives. We may also experience loss aversion when we walk away after putting many eggs into a particular basket. There can be an acute reflexive aversion to moving away from a position, especially when we sell at a significant loss.

Brain Mechanisms: The sunk cost fallacy emerges from several systems within our brains. As we research a position, our task network is engaged activating the frontal and parietal lobes. As we develop an internalized picture of the position, the default mode network activates along with

---

[12] Arkes, H.R., and C. Blumer. 1985. "The Psychology of Sunk Cost." *Organizational Behavior and Human Decision Processes* 35, no. 1, pp. 124–140.

areas involving memory and emotion in the temporal lobes. Over time, our memories of the research become permanently encoded into the cortex. At this point, it may be much more difficult to let go of a position, as memories jump to mind each time you think about it.

Our internal sense of consistency and feeling of commitment can even become enmeshed with these memories further driving a need to see things through, even as we experience losses. Evidence from functional brain imaging indicates that as sunk costs escalate, areas of the task network become increasingly engaged, as we monitor the context of the investment and engage in riskier behavior as we attempt to limit the continued losses.[13]

Overcoming the sunk cost fallacy returns us to the attention systems of the brain that we discussed in Chapter 2. The reality of poor performance on a position can sufficiently mismatch our forecast. This can trigger task mode areas to exert control and help us to pull the plug on our position before we continue to lose money.

Who's vulnerable? All investors can potentially fall victim to sunk costs. Notably, active fund managers and value investors are likely to experience this bias. Anyone attempting to short a stock must be especially vigilant of the sunk cost fallacy, as shorts will incur much greater losses if one does not exit their position promptly if things do not play out as expected. Building up a personal history with a position can lead to irrational behaviors that can inhibit failing investments from being removed from your portfolio especially when they should be.

Remedies:

- Draft a simple one-page investment summary document stating the investment case and summarizing the data that support it. This document should map out the execution of the investment with suggested actions to be taken upon various potential developments *prior to* their occurrence. This roadmap will help you to avoid making gut reaction-based decisions as events develop in the heat of the moment.

---

[13] Zeng, J., Q. Zhang, C. Chen, R. Yu, and Q. Gong. 2013. "An fMRI Study on Sunk Cost Effect." *Brain Research*, no. 1519, pp. 63–70.

- If a position has worked out well, you may over-emphasize the bullish narrative associated with the idea and undesirably interpret incoming evidence to be consistent with your original narrative. Recording your thoughts will help you to notice if this is happening.
- When you research a potential investment, you expend significant time and energy. All of this effort can lead to pressure to execute the investment, *even if it is not warranted.* Use pre-set criteria for making the investment. These may include potential upside, potential downside, management quality, operational leverage, financial leverage, cyclicality, macro exposure, and degree of uncertainty. These criteria should be scored and the investment should be compared to the existing portfolio for correlation and risk factor exposure.
- After an investment is made and circumstances change, whether it is a change in the factual circumstances surrounding the fundamentals of an investment, or simply a change in the security price, *be ready to act.*
- Limit your losses by including stop-loss rules to get you out of a situation, rather than risk throwing good money after bad.

* also see *consistency bias* and *framing bias* (Chapter 3)

No matter how far you've gone down the wrong road, turn back.
—Unknown

Affect Bias

Definition: Impressions can last, especially when they involve our emotions. When a positive or negative event occurs in the life of a position, it may impact us in ways that we cannot perceive. This is known as the *affect bias*—a heuristic, or mental shortcut, that leaves us open to distorting our thinking about a position based on our emotional history with it.
Background: The affect bias has been demonstrated in a variety of contexts where an emotional cue leaves a prolonged impression on one's attitude

toward something. This lasting impression can influence our thinking in subtle ways that may undermine portfolio performance over time.

Antoine Bechara and his colleagues at the University of Iowa developed a memorable gambling experiment to understand the relationship between reason and emotion.[14] Bechara and his colleagues presented people with four decks of cards face down and allowed them to freely choose a card from any deck. After each choice, the card was revealed as a "win" or a "loss" and an amount of money was added or subtracted from the person's total. Each deck contained a random mix of "win" and "loss" cards, but critically the amounts varied. Decks 1 and 2 were "safe" decks. These provided rather low payouts for win cards, but even lower penalties for loss cards. Meanwhile, decks 3 and 4 were "risky," as they paid out handsomely, but incurred even larger penalties on their loss cards.

Participants in the experiment began the Iowa gambling task naïve to which decks were best. They made many selections without a clue what the outcome would be. During the game, the researchers also measured players' arousal levels using a skin conductance response device hooked up to the players' hands. As players incurred losses, their arousal increased in response to the emotional feedback. Bechara and his colleagues periodically paused the game in order to ask players what their strategies were. Fascinatingly, the players frequently reported having no clear idea which decks were better, yet they already had begun to show arousal levels *before* they chose from the risky decks! In other words, their emotional systems were already bracing for potential losses even before they understood the game's probabilities. Many players developed hunches that certain decks were riskier after about 50 selections. Eventually most players consciously understood which decks were risky by the end of one-hundred card choices. This study indicates that emotional signals helped to guide people away from the risky decks prior to gaining a full understanding of their characteristics.

This research reveals two key features of the affect bias. First, our emotions are powerful, with our emotional system being so averse to losing

---

[14]   Bechara, A., H. Damasio, D. Tranel, and A.R. Damasio. 1997. "Deciding Advantageously Before Knowing the Advantageous Strategy." *Science* 275, no. 5304, pp. 1293–1295.

that it may at times be tracking outcomes better than our conscious minds. Second, the effects of emotions can persist. Imagine that the decks had swapped value at some point and now decks A and B became more risky. It would take us quite a while to become comfortable with the formerly risky decks C and D. Once bitten, twice shy.

Relevance: The affect heuristic may be relevant when a positive or negative event happens early on in an investment. Also, when bad or good news comes along it may persist in the market long after it should, which can be an opportunity if you can see this. We need to be agile when observing price movement so that we do not become fixed on an avoidance strategy due to early losses that are not truly indicative of the health of a position.

Processing Level: Affect bias is primarily an instinct bias. Emotions are a core feature of our brains and when we feel loss, we are quick to move away. Likewise, when we gain rewards, we may inappropriately feel fondly toward an investment beyond a reasonable point in time if things are going downhill.

Brain Mechanisms: The affect bias likely comes about from our emotional brain systems interacting with our conscious thinking. When Antoine Bechara and his colleagues carried out the gambling task research, they also investigated individuals who had impairments to the frontal lobes, usually from strokes, or brain injuries.[15] They investigated the emotional guidance of a group of people who had sustained damage to the ventromedial frontal lobes that are involved in linking emotion to cognition. These neurological patients often performed terribly on the task, usually losing all of their money and continuing to make risky choices throughout the game. They seemed to be insensitive to losses and also failed to appreciate the magnitude of the gains they made. These patients also failed to show the anticipatory arousal responses as measured by the skin conductance response, as uninjured players had shown. Furthermore, they continued to make risky card choices even after they could consciously report that Deck C and D were forcing them to lose money!

The gambling task research tells us that the ventral (underside) of the mid-frontal lobes is important for connecting losses and gains with the

---

[15]   Damasio, A.R. 2006. *Descartes' Error.* Random House.

emotional responses that follow. This suggests that the affect heuristic may rely upon this frontal lobe area for guiding our financial behavior. The memories of penalties appear to be particularly acute and we may inappropriately continue to devalue a good position if we happened to experience losses with it initially. Bad outcomes will follow if we do not appropriately resize positions and actively monitor pricing and research, being sure to keep an objective eye on what is occurring.

Who's vulnerable? Active fund managers, momentum, and value investors are all susceptible to the affect bias.

Remedies:

- Keep an investment journal recording the process for each investment so that you can rationally evaluate outcomes and learn from them. You should expect that the journal will be constantly amended as new lessons are learned. We suggest that your playbook should outline your process and have a guide for investing in certain industries and under certain conditions. This will help you to avoid the persistent influence of emotions that can degrade your performance.

* also see *salience bias* (Chapter 3) and *framing bias* (Chapter 3)

> *I think of myself as an intelligent, sensitive human being with the soul of a clown, which always forces me to blow it at the most important moments.*
>
> —Jim Morrison

Expectancy Bias

Definition: We actively shape what we perceive. The *expectancy bias* arises when we impose a preconceived set of expectations onto a situation. These expectations can unwittingly morph our observations making them conform to what we think we are about to witness. This process can result in faulty observations that lie somewhere between objective reality and our prior sense of what we thought was going to happen.

Background: Imagine you are about to take a kayaking trip at a coastal harbor. You casually mention the trip to a friend who tells you that there have been an usually high number of great white shark sightings there this summer. Undeterred, you head to the harbor. As you paddle along, you notice yourself constantly looking down at the water and imaging what you would do if a huge shark were to suddenly ambush you! Was that dark shadow out front of you just a reflection off the water, or was it the real life cousin of Jaws lurking beneath the surface?! You survive the trip, but remain convinced that you narrowly escaped with your life.

Had there not been mention of the frequent shark activity in the area, you would likely have experienced the same trip without any notion whatsoever of sharks. They existed in your mind only, but affected your experience in a very real way.

For many years scientists have been concerned about the role of our interpretations in corrupting our objective observations. Lucien Cordaro and James Ison demonstrated this type of expectancy bias in a classic study in 1963.[16] If you took any college level biology you might be familiar with planaria, which are very small worms that possesses remarkable powers of regeneration. Many a biology student has either examined planaria regeneration, or tried to condition them to move in certain directions. Such examinations seem simple enough, but their results are hardly straightforward. Cordaro and Ison asked student experimenters to record both the movements and turns made by planaria worms. One group was told that the worms would move and turn often, while another group was told that they would not. The students who expected high rates of movement reported approximately 18 times more movements and nearly five times as many turns compared to the group that expected little movement! Expectations dramatically impacted the observers' interpretations and biased what they thought they were seeing. For those student observers anticipating lots of activity, the expectancy bias was capable of turning a rather mundane creature into a veritable gymnast among worms.

Relevance: Expectancy bias can be insidious for investors. Once we begin to form an impression on a position, this may subsequently influence us to see what we expect to see. On a daily basis, we may start to rationalize

---

[16] Cordaro, L., and J.R. Ison. 1963. "Psychology of the Scientist: X. Observer Bias in Classical Conditioning of the Planarian." *Psychological Reports* 13, no. 3, pp. 787–789.

why price movements are not fitting our expectations and begin to systematically discount evidence that runs counter to our thesis.

Processing Level: Expectancy bias acts at both the intuition and reason
levels. We build impressions about our investments. We retrieve these
impressions each time we take in new information about the position
and they influence what we observe and interpret. The observation feels
intuitive and we have little ability to examine the bias that may be moving
us toward an expected observation over a more objective one. We then
import this intuitive biased impression into our reasoning and com-
pound the error by consciously justifying its occurrence. This can become
extremely troubling, as we can continue to strengthen our pre-existing
erroneous assumptions each time we conclude that we have been correct
all along. This can lead to adding too aggressively to profitable positions
as favorable price fluctuations are interpreted as the market validating the
investment thesis.

Brain Mechanisms: The expectancy bias results from our memory systems
and their interactions with both the default mode network and the task
network. When someone decides to invest in a particular company, they
do so because they have formed a favorable or unfavorable impression of
its future outcomes. This memory becomes encoded into our cortex and
called into an active state each time we consider the investment, or intake
new information about it. At this point, the memory of the narrative can
bias our interpretations. We fixate on news that is consistent with our
narrative, while also discounting and rationalizing away information that
counters it.

The task mode network is involved in active engagement with the
news on a position. This network is associated with reasoning through
problems and actively taking in information—things we should be doing.
The activity of this network is not sufficient for sound reasoning if we
also call to mind previous conclusions that bias our interpretation of new
incoming data.

Who's vulnerable? This bias is pervasive among just about every type of
active investor. As with other memory biases, when we form personal
connections to a position then we can no longer examine it without
retrieving a previous conclusion.

Remedies:

- When preparing a pre-mortem for an investment idea (see Chapter 8), you should emphasize the risks and provide them with a probabilistic assessment of success and note potential alternatives outcomes and their likely impact on the valuation of the security you are reviewing. This practice will help to ensure that you remain open to alternate interpretations as they may arise and do not become blinded by expectations that your bullish assessment will eventually and inevitably play out as you see it.

- Acknowledge that a position is a desirable bet, but that it may not produce a desirable outcome if the risks come to fruition. You may also mention that your opinion could change as things develop. Having voiced alternative and unfavorable outcomes, you may reduce your tendency to over-search for your preferred outcome. You will also guard against becoming over-committed and seeing what you expect to see according to your favored narrative.

- Sometimes it helps to say that this is your opinion based on the facts as you see them, but also remind others that your opinion could change at any time if you acquire other information, or if the hand of fate tips to favor the risks in your assessment.

- You may also want to review the position upon certain designated milestones or catalysts that you designate in your pre-mortem. This will give you a pre-set time to reconsider the possible variant alternative outcomes in the context of events that have occurred since your initial investment decision.

* also see *consistency bias* and *framing bias* (Chapter 3)

I fully expected that, by the end of the century, we would have achieved substantially more than we actually did.

—Neil Armstrong

PART III

CHAPTER 6

Knowledge

Acquiring and Updating Knowledge

Thus far we have discussed how attention and memory selectively highlight certain information to the exclusion of other details. We regularly distort incoming information to meet our current purposes. Our recollections reflect and amplify these distortions. In this third section we will discuss the role of our knowledge in altering our focus.

Knowledge spans the gap between attention and memory. It is built up over a lifetime and it actively shapes our focus of attention. We often have little ability to guide how we use our knowledge. Rather, our knowledge frequently guides us and does so very automatically. This strong effect of knowledge on investment performance can make its influence either a blessing or a curse depending on the circumstances. At its worst, our knowledge can hinder our performance by getting in our way and generating a narrative that is misfit to the situation. These misfit narratives tend to feel right at first, as they possess some surface similarities between the current conditions and prior ones. Over the longer term, we can begin to see the gaps as ongoing events no longer fit the narrative, but often this occurs too late to change course.

The Brain as a Pattern Matching System

Your brain helps you to efficiently process information to get through your day. You engage with the world around you, take in new information, make sense of it, and translate it into action. Pattern recognition helps our brains to act efficiently. In a complex and dynamic world, our brains find patterns and group them. Identifying patterns allows us to take shortcuts by acting in similar ways toward whole sets of information. We gain speed and accuracy through this process; however, with this efficiency comes the possibility that we become *too active* in pattern finding and this can lead us to convince ourselves that there is meaning in random data. Some of these cases lead to predictable biases.

Emerging brain science suggests that our neurons activate in predictable patterns when we solve problems. An illustrative example of this principle was reported by Theodore Berger and his colleagues, who successfully "transplanted" a neuron-based pattern into rat's brains to help with cognitive performance.[1] The researchers trained rats to solve a memory-based matching task and recorded the activity patterns of neurons within an area of the hippocampus, a key memory region. This data source enabled the researchers to isolate a neural pattern for successful task performance. They then blocked memory formation using a chemical injected into the brain. Using electrodes, the researchers successfully input neural patterns back into the brain. Remarkably, the recipients of the neural patterns were better at the task! The correct pattern from earlier was able to help the rat to perform at the key moment when it had been re-inserted into the brain.

Our brains code information into patterns over time. When the same context occurs repeatedly, our brains establish larger and more elaborate patterns. These can become so well-established that they enable fast and highly automatic behaviors. Our brains build in biases that are evoked by familiar contexts and these help us to be highly efficient with our time and energy. We can operate effectively using our intuition because of these patterns. Challenges can arise when we make intuitive financial decisions that are based heavily upon automatic and intuitive thinking, rather than sound, reasoned analysis. Don't trust that a successful pattern observed in the past will always bear fruit later on when circumstances may have changed.

---

[1] Berger, T.W., R.E. Hampson, D. Song, A. Goonawardena, V.Z. Marmarelis, and S.A. Deadwyler. 2011. "A Cortical Neural Prosthesis for Restoring and Enhancing Memory." *Journal of Neural Engineering* 8, no. 4, p. 046017.

Our intuition about the future is linear. But the reality of information technology is exponential, and that makes a profound difference. If I take 30 steps linearly, I get to 30. If I take 30 steps exponentially, I get to a billion.

—Ray Kurzweil

Learning Systems in the Brain

In the first half of the 20th century, the field of behavioral psychology focused almost exclusively on the study of learning. All manner of experiments were carried out with pigeons and rats, which learned to run mazes and peck keys in order to obtain small bits of food. The task context was usually new to the animal (meaning past knowledge did not influence performance). Often the animal's goal was to simply obtain the most food available through whatever new action was required by the experimenter. Rodents and pigeons proved to be highly flexible learners and highly sensitive to probabilities in their environment.

The brain systems involved in learning are increasingly well-understood and are highly relevant to investing. We have already discussed several of these brain areas in Chapters 2 and 4. The regions of the basal ganglia are sensitive to rewards and respond to expectations about successes as well. Our basal ganglia act as probability detectors reading the contingencies and statistics that we encounter within our environment. We discussed the hippocampus, a memory-related structure in Chapter 4. Like the basal ganglia, the hippocampus is involved in coding the structure of our environment as we learn. Hippocampal neurons respond during navigation toward landmarks, sights, and sounds. Rats and pigeons can stay remarkably well fed in a laboratory using these brain circuits to learn.

While we too have a basal ganglia and hippocampus, we are capable of learning quite differently than other species. We embellish and add a lot of our own structure to our learning. We can see beyond the immediate sensory data in the environment, due to our ability to store lengthy narratives as they play out over time. People actively sculpt their mental models by noticing similarities and differences among widely different environments separated by time and involving different people. We are sensitive to the abstract structure of a situation and we have the ability to theorize and run experiments to validate (or invalidate) our ideas. This active intake and consideration of information allows us to persist in our activities, sometimes for the better, as we accurately read a complicated narrative, sometimes for the worse, if we fail to notice contrary feedback.

> *The practice of narrative and argument does not lead to invention, but it compels a certain coherence of thought.*
>
> —Jean Piaget

Structuring Knowledge in the Brain

We are highly active and dynamic thinkers. We constantly form conscious impressions of the world around us, take in new information, and then revisit our impressions. Our brains allow us to structure our environment and actively shape our world through our actions over time.

The frontal lobes play a strong role in storing our structured representations of the environment. Researcher, Jordan Grafman refers to the frontal lobes as guiding us via *structured-event complexes*, which are rich brain networks representing events and situations. Grafman has theorized that these complexes enable people to store elaborate situational representations distributed across the cortex.[2] If a situation involves visualization, the network representing it likely invokes areas of visual cortex. Likewise, verbal memory networks would involve areas of the auditory cortex. An expert Blackjack player would access structured-event complexes that include these features plus input on risk, odds, and strategy. Just as brain plasticity enables us to modify our memories, these elaborated narratives can be called forward into consciousness and modified with experience as well.

Our structured knowledge is frequently called a *schema*. Schemas were introduced in the research community many decades ago by Sir Frederick Bartlett, a visionary researcher who worked on complex knowledge in the early 20th century. This was a time when much of the field was exclusively concerned with studying simpler learning in animals. In one of

---

[2] Grafman, J., F. Krueger, E. Morsella, J.A. Bargh, and P.M. Gollwitzer. 2009. *The Prefrontal Cortex Stores Structured Event Complexes that are the Representational Basis for Cognitively Derived Actions*. Oxford Handbook of Human Action.

Bartlett's famous experiments, he presented people with a tale of tribal warfare called *The War of the Ghosts*.[3] This short narrative described many routine events in native warfare, such as taking canoes down the river to attack another tribe with arrows. The story also included some distinctly odd details, such as someone being struck by an arrow without pain and the notion that the warriors were ghosts. Bartlett found that people had accurate memories of the story when he tested them minutes-to-hours after hearing it. He then tested people months-to-years later and found that their recollections of the story had drifted off course in predictable ways. These changes are characteristic of how our brains alter knowledge over time. Bartlett reported the following:

1. People retained the main structure of the narrative.
2. People forgot many of the minor and unusual details.
3. People added information that was not present in the original story.

This last finding is especially relevant. People's embellishments to the story tended to fit with their broader general impressions of tribal warfare. Details about travel in a canoe, bows and arrows, and invasions were easy for people to generate, since these are common elements in other familiar legends and narratives from history.

We develop schemas for a variety of situations in life. As an exercise, take a glance at the photo in Figure 6.1. Now close the book for a moment and try to remember everything you can from that image. When most people try this they immediately recall the most common features found in offices (chairs, a desk, a computer). Once you get past those core elements, you may recall some unique items on a shelf, or desktop. You are unlikely to recall much about the color scheme, the details of any office plants, or the arrangement of papers on the desk. Our brains guide us through use of a heavily filtered version of the situation that we have experienced. The end result is that our knowledge guides us toward representing our circumstances in ways that are consistent with what we notice much of the time.

3   Bartlett, F.C. 1932. *Remembering: An Experimental and Social Study.* Cambridge: Cambridge University.

Figure 6.1 We often store the gist of a situation, but lose the specific details

Filtering World Knowledge

We cannot possibly gather all of the relevant data available, so we are limited to a partial view of things. This is the essence of a term researchers call *embodied cognition*, a field that studies how our physical structure filters our experience and our schemas. Our brains are highly interactive within our environments. We tend to think that our brains are running the show, but this perspective has its limits. Just as intelligence does not exist in a vacuum, we do not passively take in all information and process it. You are not a brain in a jar. You experience the world through a perspective influenced by the configuration of your body and sensory systems.

The embodied cognition perspective explains why some devices feel more intuitive than others. Our brains are pre-wired with some biases based on the orientation or our bodies and the fact that we do so much with our hands. A savvy car dashboard designer can configure the instruments in a way that facilitates our driving. This is accomplished by *using* our brains' biases to guide designs that make our lives easier. Smart investing is often more complex and ambiguous than driving. Therefore, if you rely on the easy path guided by your prior knowledge, you can find yourself relying too much on biased thinking and thereby fail to leverage nuanced opportunities.

Effective investment research requires gathering the most relevant current knowledge about a company in order to make accurate predictions about what will happen next. It is important to keep in mind that events will unfold in a way that is filtered by the brain. We cannot see time horizons in the long distant future. Such timescales tend to be incompatible with our brains' quick reward-based incentive processing systems. Therefore, it is helpful to try to step back and consider how things might look from another perspective, one with more information and fewer processing limits.

Priming the Pump

Our knowledge can subtly guide us without our awareness. Try this quick exercise:

1. Quickly think of a tool
2. Quickly think of an animal
3. Quickly think of a color

If you are like most people, then you probably provided rather consistent answers. The tool category likely resulted in either a hammer or a screwdriver. The animal was probably a dog, or perhaps a cat. The color was likely red or blue. These are predictable associations for most people because they are extremely common examples of each category. The statistical machinery within our brains seizes upon probabilities and regularities out in the environment. Fast and effortless associations jump to mind constantly as we move through our daily lives. These associations guide us and shape our mental shortcuts. The more common and consistent an association, the more automatic it becomes in our minds. At the extremes, this is exactly what we mean by bias—an association so rapid and effortless that we cannot prevent it from leaping into our minds and influencing our behavior.

Psychological Priming

Priming is the term psychological researchers use to describe the fast and automatic influence of prior information. Just as you can prime an engine by pumping a small amount of fuel into the line to ease ignition, your brain's perceptual system sends out a brief shot of energy through the relevant brain network of associations that allows us to more quickly ignite a memory or action when needed.

Imagine that you are in a psychology lab and asked to judge words as quickly as possible. The researchers present you with high associate priming words that will make you ready to judge the next word quickly. For example, if you just read "dog" and then had to judge if "cat" was a word or not, you would do so faster than if you saw "dog" and judged the word "avocado." The speed advantage of judging "cat" comes from the fact that exposure to the word "dog" primes the *household pets* network of your brain. Your neurons can then zero in on the "cat" judgment milliseconds faster than you would if you were asked this question out of the blue. Your reaction to "avocado" occurs as usual, as dogs are weakly associated with this fruit (believe it or not an avocado really is a fruit, despite what your vegetable network may be telling you).

The priming phenomenon may explain why experts appear to perform so effortlessly, even under pressure. When an expert has seen things before, they will quickly notice the relevance and call to mind a highly probable successful action. They do not need to devote much attention and effort to this process, as effective answers materialize automatically.

> *When you revolutionize education, you're taking the very mechanism of how people get smarter and do new things, and you're priming the pump for so many incredible things.*
>
> —Bill Gates

Beware of Easy Answers

By this point in the book, you probably already notice a problem emerging with all this talk of easy and automatic thinking. The challenge with fast and effortless associations is that we frequently fail to question them. Sensible answers come to mind effortlessly, so they feel intuitively correct.

Once you get into this mode there is a temptation to play things "fast and loose." It can feel burdensome to step back and question your actions. The reality is that this is precisely the time to exercise caution. In Chapter 8, we will discuss strategies that you can enact to help you minimize the undue influence of these knowledge-based biases. We all need external checks and balances, as automatic thinking is one of the primary culprits of potentially crippling financial biases.

You might imagine that novice investors will need this advice more, but surprisingly experts can face even greater challenges that come along with quick and easy answers. Knowledge builds up over time in complex brain networks. The more experience you feed your brain, the stronger a given association network becomes. Eventually the network can become hardened and resistant to change. This means that it takes particularly dramatic counter-evidence to inspire an expert to question their assumptions.

Distorted Perception

A classic perception study demonstrated our remarkable ability to adapt to new conditions. In this procedure, people wear specialized goggles that flip all of the incoming visual information. The goggles make it so that the floor appears to be the ceiling and vice-versa. Early psychologist, George Stratton reported on his experiences wearing inversion lenses in the 1890s.[4] Stratton initially struggled to function, navigating around his house looking at everything upside down. In addition to feeling nausea and discomfort, Stratton was clumsy and anxious, as he bumped into objects and experienced surprise at the mismatch between his vision and physical senses. He wore the inversion lenses for eight consecutive days with each day getting better than the last. By the end of the experiment, he no longer felt anxious, he was much more fluid in navigating the upside-down world of his perception, and found that he had adapted to the once foreign visual environment. This story has an unusual twist: after removing these trick lenses, Stratton struggled once again with clumsiness and a distorted environment—this time generated merely by the mismatch between his

---

[4]   Stratton, G.M. 1897. "Vision Without Inversion of the Retinal Image." *Psychological Review* 4, no. 4, p. 341.

internal expectations and what his own eyes were showing him. Over a century later, this remains a landmark experiment demonstrating how the brain can adapt to distortion and begin to perceive it as normal.

We adapt our mental models to fit our expectations and then impose those expectations on incoming information. Our schemas can also become like a pair of glasses that distort reality. When one wears the glasses for a long time, most incoming evidence can be warped to fit the pre-existing expectations of the viewer. The distortion likely comes about from systematically increasing attention and weight on ideas consistent with expectations, while also downgrading and ignoring ideas that do not fit expectations. The result can be an idea possessing a false level of coherence with seemingly little negative evidence to counter it. Again, active steps can be put into place to avoid this type of distortion.

Preview of Knowledge Biases

We next turn our attention to the third set of biases—those based on our previous knowledge and expectations. We will initially discuss biases that are based on our individual knowledge. Such biases come about because of a gap, or a mismatch between what we know and what is really occurring out in the world. These biases frequently stem from our intuition, which in turn can alter the course of our deliberative reasoning. Secondly we discuss group decision biases. These include *groupthink*, a set of biases involving all three levels of instinct, intuition, and reason, as we make decisions and reason with our colleagues. Like individual biases, we can sometimes develop communal knowledge in groups that contains unhealthy distortions of reality.

To avoid these challenges, it is necessary to exercise care in your practices. Some important methods to address knowledge biases include actively remaining open-minded to evidence that counters a favored narrative. This may involve speaking to colleagues who hold an alternate view, or building in practices that regularly force you to question your assumptions. These strategies are discussed in association with each individual bias and are re-visited in Chapter 8 on best practices for avoiding bias. As with the previous two classes of biases, the interaction of our knowledge with incoming information relies upon our *instinct, intuition,* and *reason* skills.

Summary

- Our knowledge spans the gap between our attention and memory and is built up over a lifetime.
- Knowledge actively shapes our focus of attention and we have limited ability to guide how we use it.
- Our brains find patterns and group them automatically.
- Identifying patterns allows us to take shortcuts by acting similarly toward whole sets of information, gaining speed and accuracy.
- Over-active pattern searching can lead us to find meaning that does not actually exist in incoming information.
- People actively form mental models (representations of reality) by noticing similarities and differences among repeatedly encountered environments and situations. These form our schemas about the world.
- The frontal lobes play a major role in matching our expectations to our current place in the world.
- Embodied cognition describes how our physical structure influences our experience as our brains interact with our environment.
- Priming describes the fast and automatic influence of prior information on our current thinking.
- There is a challenge with fast associations—it is difficult to realize when they are incorrect.

Further Reading

Tulving, E., and D.L. Schacter. 1990. "Priming and Human Memory Systems." *Science* 247, no. 4940, pp. 301–306.

Chi, M.T., R. Glaser, and M.J. Farr. 2014. *The Nature of Expertise*. Psychology Press, 2014.

There is an almost universal quest for easy answers and half-baked solutions. Nothing pains some people more than having to think.

—Martin Luther King, Jr.

CHAPTER 7

Knowledge Biases

Biases Caused by What We Know

Sometimes what we know matches a particular investing context, while other times we impose incorrect patterns onto a situation to our peril. We first discuss ways that our own knowledge, or perception of our knowledge, can influence our thinking. We then discuss two important social knowledge biases that derive from our interactions with other people.

Real knowledge is to know the extent of one's ignorance.

—Confucius

I'm no genius, but I'm smart in spots and I stay around those spots.

—Tom Watson

I. Individual Knowledge Biases

There is no substitute for a well-developed body of knowledge in most walks of life. Sound investment decisions in individual businesses require a thorough knowledge of the company, the industry it participates in, and many other potentiating factors. While knowledge confers an undoubted advantage, there are times when it comes with a significant price.

Deep knowledge about any subject can leave us open to a class of biases that stem from knowing too much. These are cases in which we begin to overreach on our assumptions because we believe things are going to play out just as we have seen many times before. This can lead us to become mentally lazy, a state where we fail to sufficiently question ourselves. Some of these biases stem from assuming that we understand things more than we do, while others occur because we become blind to key information based on our substantial degree of knowledge. Let's examine some of these critical knowledge biases.

> *The doorstep to the temple of wisdom is a knowledge of our own ignorance.*
>
> —Benjamin Franklin

The Curse of Knowledge

Definition: Imagine you are bidding on a classic car at an auction. The engine does not start, but you noticed that it had a relatively simple issue with the sparkplugs that could easily be remedied. The engine looked sound otherwise. Should you bid early and high to try to run off competitors? Or should you play it cool and bid late pretending that you are begrudgingly buying a clunker for parts? Maybe others also know this is a hidden gem and are trying similar deceptive tactics.

We can get our minds spinning in circles when we try to anticipate whether someone else knows something that we know. If you know the engine looks good, then it can feel as if everyone in the auction also shares this knowledge and is waiting to pounce on this fantastic deal just as you are.

Sometimes we need to ignore a portion of the information that we possess in order to appropriately predict the value that others will place on a company. The *curse of knowledge* occurs when we make erroneous predictions about other peoples' thoughts and actions based on personal information that only we have. It is a case of our own knowledge getting in the way of our ability to make an accurate forecast about what other people, who lack that same knowledge, are likely to do. We have a difficult time ignoring our extra insight, so we act assuming others are wiser than they actually are.

Background: Economists Colin Camerer, George Loewenstein, and Martin Weber originally described this bias.[1] They asked business school finance students to play a stock trading game. The students bought and

---

[1] Camerer, C., G. Loewenstein, and M. Weber. 1989. "The Curse of Knowledge in Economic Settings: An Experimental Analysis." *Journal of political Economy* 97, no. 5, pp. 1232–1254.

sold shares, requiring them to anticipate others' assessments of value. The students provided initial earnings predictions based on company reports. Months later, the researchers provided a new group of students with the report *with* earnings numbers. These more informed students then traded assets that paid a dividend based on the initial (earnings-naïve) students' estimates. The fully informed trading group knew that the dividends were based on the naïve students predictions and should have acted accordingly by pretending that they did not know the actual earnings numbers. Despite being wise to the details, the fully-informed students fell victim to the curse of knowledge and traded as if the naïve student predictions had included pricing details. They could not avoid the influence of their own personal information when trying to estimate what less-informed people would do.

Relevance: Successful investing requires us to find gaps between our own knowledge and that of Wall Street. If you possess an informational advantage, it is important to properly estimate the degree to which the current price is either under- or over-valued. This requires calculating the magnitude of impact that your informational edge is likely to give you relative to other players in the market. The curse of knowledge phenomenon suggests that we often underestimate the gap between what we know and what other market actors know.

George Baxter once invested in an illiquid company that was benefiting from little known favorable developments that he perceived would soon become widely understood by the market. He noticed that the stock rose dramatically as he purchased shares. He imagined that other market participants had also noticed what he had and that a tailwind was driving the price up. It looked to be a large opportunity, so George took an aggressive position. Ultimately, he realized that automated algorithm trading was responsible for the additional purchasing. In effect, he had been competing with himself! He stopped buying and the price fell rapidly. The curse of knowledge led him to believe that other investors were behaving similarly because they must have seen what he did.

Processing Level: The curse of knowledge operates at the intuition and reason levels. Like other knowledge biases, it is a case of our intuition misguiding us. We fail to properly discount others' estimates based on information that only we possess.

Brain Mechanisms: The curse of knowledge involves inadequately anticipating what other people are thinking. Neuroscientists call this *perspective taking*, which involves simulating what it would be like to see the
world through the eyes of another person and access their knowledge. The
default mode network areas of the brain are frequently activated when we
think internally about our own knowledge.

Researchers Meghana Bhatt and Colin Camerer investigated perspective taking in an economic exchange game using brain imaging.[2] They
asked people to make strategic choices during the game. They compared
players' personal choices to their predictions about what the other player
would do, as well as their guesses about what the other player thought
they would do. This final act of anticipating what another person likely
thinks about your own actions is critical to the ability to anticipate what
others will do based on incomplete information (the precise conditions
for the curse of knowledge). The posterior cingulate cortex, an important
node within the default mode network, was most active in representing
the player's own choice of strategy. This region showed significantly lower
activity associated with predicting another person's strategy. The *reflected*
condition (predicting what another person thinks you will do) evoked
a posterior cingulate activity level between one's own belief and that of
another person. In other words, the act of predicting what another person
will do fell somewhere between that associated with representing oneself
and the likely strategy someone else would use. This finding suggests a
knowledge gap that leads us toward bias.

Who's vulnerable? Anyone seeking an informational advantage can fall
victim to the curse of knowledge, as they impute their knowledge on
others and fail to appropriately appreciate the market's ignorance. This
may apply particularly in cases where liquidity constraints result in the
investor's purchase and sale decisions are sufficient to influence a security's
price. This can then seem to reinforce the perception that other market
participants possess knowledge of the undiscounted factor that the investor is trying to capitalize on.

---

[2]   Bhatt, M., and C.F. Camerer. 2005. "Self-Referential Thinking and Equilib-
rium as States of Mind in Games: fMRI Evidence." *Games and Economic Behavior*
52, no. 2, pp. 424–459.

Remedies:

- After researching a given investment prospect, proceed to execute in accordance with the investment roadmap. This will help to limit your assumptions about others as you continue to gain additional knowledge.
- Remember that the price of the investment will fluctuate. This fluctuation can serve as a sort of Rorschach test for an investment manager. As you see price fluctuation, you may assume that others see what you see, or that negative (or positive) developments are being recognized by other investors. Keep in mind that you should not over-interpret price movement.
- Perhaps the simplest remedy is to hand the investment to your trader or broker with instructions on how to execute. He or she will not over-think things the way that you may.
- Stagger purchases for illiquid stocks, buy small positions aggressively, and act patiently to see if the initial momentum created by your purchases persists before adding continuously and essentially bidding yourself up.

* also see *confirmation bias* and *hindsight bias* (Chapter 3)

> *While physics and mathematics may tell us how the universe began, they are not much use in predicting human behavior because there are far too many equations to solve.*
>
> —Stephen Hawking

Anchoring Bias

Definition: Any time a price, quantity, or value has been voiced, it can powerfully distort our thinking. *Anchoring* was one of the original biases described by Amos Tversky and Daniel Kahneman. It occurs when an initial number has an oversized influence upon our subsequent actions.

Background: Anchoring bias was initially described as a heuristic, or guideline, that people use in order to efficiently get through their work. Anchor values are associated with two main dangers: (1) people do not adequately scrutinize the basis for the anchor point, or it's appropriateness to the situation, (2) people then fail to adjust adequately up or down from the anchor point.

In one of Tversky and Kahneman's colorful examples, they asked people to quickly estimate the product of complicated multiplication problems after only five seconds of thought.[3] One group of students estimated the product of an ascending sequence (1 x 2 x 3 x 4 x 5 x 6 x 7 x 8), while another group estimated the same problem presented in descending order (8 x 7 x 6 x 5 x 4 x 3 x 2 x 1). The limited time permitted only a ballpark estimate of the product and the ordering produced dramatic differences. People estimating based on the ascending sequence produced a number around 512, while the descending sequence led to an estimate of 2,250! Both groups were also well off from the correct answer of 40,320. In five seconds, people could only multiply a few numbers, thereby producing far too small an estimate. People appeared to have anchored on that initial value and then inadequately adjusted their estimation upward.

Another challenge with anchoring is that people often fail to notice that an anchor may be unfounded or inappropriate. In that same article, Kahneman and Tversky described a time that they asked people to estimate the percentage of African countries that are members of the United Nations. Prior to estimating, the researchers spun a wheel bearing the numbers 1 to 100, providing an anchor value that was obviously irrelevant. The wheel's random number was enough to sway the subsequent judgments. For example, people who saw the wheel settle on the number 10 suggested that roughly 25 percent of countries are in the U.N., while those who saw the wheel spin out a 65, guessed 45 percent of countries. This striking example indicates that people will gravitate toward anchors, even when they are clearly arbitrary.

Relevance: Some transactions involve goods or services of ambiguous value, so we haggle to arrive at a fair price. Where to begin when negotiating? Typically the buyer makes the initial offer. Lowball initial offers risk offending sellers and blocking the transaction. Respectable initial offers allow the negotiation to proceed. A savvy buyer will issue the lowest

---

[3] Tversky, A., and D. Kahneman. 1974. "Judgment Under Uncertainty: Heuristics and Biases." *Science* 185, no. 4157, pp. 1124–1131.

number possible without offending. Once the seller engages, then the whole negotiation is merely an adjustment up from that initial anchor point.

Stock pricing is an exercise in putting numbers on value, so the risk of anchoring is very high. The best opportunities are likely to be found when the price is far off from the true value of a company, so investors must be vigilant to avoid overly fixating on a current price, thereby failing to predict how much price may move simply because of the current level. *Processing Level:* Anchoring is an intuition bias. In a world that requires subjective estimates, we tend to grab onto any number that is forthcoming. Like the confirmation bias discussed later in this chapter, the introduction of a number can result in an outsized influence, even when it is not well-suited to the situation.

Brain Mechanisms: Anchor values likely take hold because we are acutely sensitive to the context of our decisions. An anchor value serves as a piece of evidence, often unfounded, that we assimilate into our predictions about what should happen next. There are times when we should adjust more dramatically from the anchor and times when we should discard the anchor altogether, but we are reluctant to do so after our brains integrate it into our mental sketch of the situation.

One reason for our reluctance to adjust is that our brains are engaged in a calculation process with uncertain values when we fall victim to anchoring bias. Neuroscientists Diana Tamir and Jason Mitchell investigated anchoring biases using brain imaging.[4] They asked people to provide ratings for a variety of characteristics (fears about public speaking, enjoyment of skiing, and so on). People in the experiment rated their own feelings on the topic and also estimated of how others would likely feel about these same situations. An area in the middle of the frontal lobes involved in the default mode network was active in response to the differences between self-ratings and those for other people. In other words, the middle frontal cortex became more active when people moved farther away from their anchor point (how they personally felt about the situations).

---

[4]   Tamir, D.I., and J.P. Mitchell. 2010. "Neural Correlates of Anchoring-and-Adjustment During Mentalizing." *Proceedings of the National Academy of Sciences* 107, no. 24, pp. 10827–10832.

This finding indicates that our frontal lobes carry out an estimation process that is calibrated by our personal anchor points. Decision contexts rich in detail should allow for more accurate calibration, while those sparse in detail leave us open to inappropriately using an arbitrary anchor point. Anchoring bias tends to occur most frequently in the investment process when investors review sell-side analyst assumptions about future earnings and price targets for securities they are reviewing. Once those projections are reviewed, it is likely that the investor's own assessments will cluster around the sell-side projections.

Who's vulnerable? Investors are likely to fall victim to anchoring bias because positions have clear prices. Once a security has been labeled with a value, it is very difficult to adjust appropriately off of this numerical anchor. Spotting great opportunities requires an ability to uncover underlying value that is not yet priced into the stock. Anchoring bias can occur when investors focus too much on price and fail to adequately consider causal factors driving price.

Remedies:

- Reviewing sell-side commentary only *after* completing your own fundamental research offers you the opportunity to mitigate anchoring bias. By reviewing this research early in your process, you risk anchoring on the sell-side's estimates, so save any review of others' analysis to the end of your fundamental research process.

- Be aware that you could become anchored on your own conclusions after you complete your financial modeling. Strive to avoid a static analysis that assumes only one possible outcome. Rather, try to develop multiple scenarios that factor in the outcomes of various risks and make an assessment in each case.

- As you monitor an investment, or potential investment, revisit earlier assumptions and adjust them when new developments occur.

- Use anchoring to your advantage: Investors often focus on small changes to estimates of future returns despite substantive changes that require larger adjustments to expectations. Often, such an adjustment will only be priced in after two-to-three new data points. If you can make an accurate assessment early on, then you can beat the crowd and adjust the investment prior to the market fully appreciating the magnitude of the shift.

* also see *confirmation bias*

A good decision is based on knowledge and not on numbers.

—Plato

Confirmation Bias

Definition: When you develop an investment theory it is common for your opinion to harden over time. As evidence mounts you begin to take for granted that your investment theory will unfold as expected. Eventually, you reach a point of no return where you reflexively discount evidence that conflicts with your investment theory and keep justifying why every bit of news is consistent with your thesis. This is known as the *confirmation bias*, a situation where evidence for a favored hypothesis is cherry-picked, while counter-evidence is discounted, or outright ignored. *Background:* Good scientific inquiry guides us to design an experiment in a way that could potentially *falsify* a possible explanation, or hypothesis. Repeated affirmation of a specific explanation simply provides a larger degree of support for that narrative. The key to progress in reasoning is to refute a possibility, thereby eliminating a potential cause-effect sequence. This helps us home in on the reality of a situation.

Psychological researcher Peter Wason described a classic illustration of *confirmation bias.*[5] Wason was keenly interested in the quirks of human nature and how they affect our reasoning. In a particularly clever experiment, he gave people a sequence of three numbers: 2–4–6 and told them that the series fit a secret rule. Next, people tried to figure out the rule by proposing their own sequences of three numbers. Wason would provide

---

[5] Wason, P.C. 1960. "On the Failure to Eliminate Hypotheses in a Conceptual Task." *Quarterly Journal of Experimental Psychology* 12, no. 3, pp. 129–140.

feedback as to whether a proposed sequence fit his rule. Most people generated many sequences and arrived at a plausible rule and most were wrong. Often the hypothesized rule was detailed and sophisticated, for example "ascending progression formed by adding or multiplying by a constant," or "the second number is the first number plus one and the third is the first number plus four." The actual secret rule was the comically simple "any ascending number sequence." Nearly everyone had overthought the problem.

We tend to anchor onto a hypothesis and then seek out confirmatory evidence for it, rather than seeking to break the theory in order to improve it. We are quite quick to verify a hypothesis, but much more reluctant to search for evidence that could potentially derail a current theory.

Relevance: Confirmation bias is one of the most insidious knowledge biases that plagues investors. We have to start somewhere and a thorough analysis can often yield what appears to be a sound forecast. Committing to a particular position on a stock often means going out on a limb and going against the grain. The prevailing opinion may not fit your thesis, but you need commit to it regardless. The challenge with this commitment is that we are generally biased to notice information that validates our position, not information that invalidates it. This can lead to a blindness toward new information that would cast doubt upon a prevailing thesis.

Processing Level: Confirmation bias acts at the level of intuition. It feels good to be right and we can become blind to alternatives when things look like they are falling in line with our thinking. This biased viewpoint can lead us to inappropriately discount relevant information countering our preferred thesis. We are often unaware of this tendency.

Brain Mechanisms: Confirmation bias develops from an interaction between incoming information and prior knowledge. It typically takes you some time to understand a new situation in which you are confronted with rewards or penalties for particular actions. The basal ganglia learning circuitry helps us to sort out which actions to take based on reward probabilities. People can override this learning process simply by having a prior idea in mind. When we are heavily guided by an expectation, we no longer take the time to listen to our basal ganglia. Rather, we distort the evidence to fit with our expectations.

Bradley Doll and his colleagues performed an investigation the confirmation bias linked to our genes.[6] People vary in their ability to utilize the brain chemical dopamine. Some people have a genetic tendency to process dopamine more efficiently in the prefrontal cortex compared to others. The researchers asked people to decide between two options to maximize rewards. In a tricky move, the researchers misled people in advance about which choice was better. People with more frontal dopamine activity were more susceptible to the confirmation bias and persisted in following the bogus rule longer. Meanwhile, people who are genetically prone to less efficient dopamine use (and less frontal lobe guidance) were quicker to abandon the inaccurate prior information. This facilitated their ability to learn the true reward contingencies via their basal ganglia learning systems.

This study shows us that our frontal lobes can steer us astray when we think we know what will happen next and more effective frontal lobe guidance can mislead us more effectively!

Who's vulnerable? The confirmation bias is pervasive across all active investors. Those who develop a strong thesis and great conviction take on additional risk of being incorrect. Investors who have gone public with their predictions and people who have held a position for a long time may be especially prone to this bias, as their mental engagement with the position may strengthen their confidence and undermine their ability to adjust to unforeseen unfolding information that runs counter to their thesis.

Remedies:
- Have regular conversations with someone who adopts a Devil's advocate position. This exercise can help you to avoid applying the blinders and seeking only confirmatory evidence. Also, talking to others who are experts in an area can help to avoid this bias as well, as they will likely offer new insights.
- Think in percentages rather than right and wrong and adjust based on incremental unfolding information. Negative out-

6   Doll, B.B., K.E. Hutchison, and M.J. Frank. 2011. "Dopaminergic Genes Predict Individual Differences in Susceptibility to Confirmation Bias." *Journal of Neuroscience* 31, no. 16, pp. 6188–6198.

comes should undermine your confidence in a narrative and
influence you to re-consider your position.

- Imagine alternate universes where things can always
  unfold differently based on a multitude of potentially
  interactive factors. There is rarely only ever one inevitable
  outcome.

- Conduct pre- and post-mortem evaluations of your investments. The pre-mortem is especially valuable for avoiding
  confirmation bias. Develop multiple scenarios and try to
  identify a factor, or factors, that can make you lose. This will
  help you to notice these if they occur.

- Keep an investment journal and re-visit your initial narrative
  paying particular attention to notice gaps between that situation and your current thinking.

- Beware of the investment positions that you are most confident in. Confidence has a way of blinding us to alternate
  unseen possibilities.

- Regularly ask yourself whether you may be overly discounting counter-evidence because it is inconsistent with what
  you want to happen. Pay attention to counter-evidence
  and note that if the bulk of incoming information favors a
  new emerging thesis, then you should reduce your position
  accordingly.

- Use inductive reasoning by starting out with the facts absent
  of any general theory, then draw conclusions based on your
  observations. Be mindful that the world is a fluid place and
  you should be suspicious of certainty.

- In team-based investing, the group should meet during the
  initial analysis phase to review the analysts' pitch. Each team
  member should independently assess the potential for the
  position to succeed and to fail. These evaluations will help to
  maximize diversity of opinion and desirable disagreements
  that can better inform the ultimate decision maker, who will
  likely have his or her own perspective.

* also see *anchoring bias*

Being deeply knowledgeable on one subject narrows one's focus and increases confidence, but it also blurs dissenting views until they are no longer visible, thereby transforming data collection into bias confirmation and morphing self-deception into self-assurance.

—Michael Shermer

Base-Rate Neglect

Definition: When we estimate probabilities it is tempting to evaluate just the incoming facts and focus only on what is taking place in the short term. This reliance on initial impressions and shallow analysis leaves us open to neglecting additional key information about probabilities. *Base-rate neglect* occurs when we fail to consider the general likelihood of specific events that we consider.

Background: Amos Tversky and Daniel Kahneman studied people's probability estimates and reported the base-rate neglect phenomenon.[7] They observed this during judgments involving both numerical base-rate information and specific individual information. For example, they told people that they would be reading descriptions of individuals who were drawn from a sample of 70 lawyers and 30 engineers. One of the descriptions follows below:

> *Jack is a 45-year-old man. He is married and has four children. He is generally conservative, careful, and ambitious. He shows no interest in political and social issues and spends most of his free time on his many hobbies, which include home carpentry, sailing, and mathematical puzzles.*

Most people over-estimated the chances chance that Jack was one of the engineers in the sample. The fact that Jack was contained in a sample with only 30 percent engineers was overshadowed by his stereotypical engineer

---

[7] Tversky, A., and D. Kahneman. 1973. "Availability: A Heuristic for Judging Frequency and Probability." *Cognitive Psychology* 5, no. 2, pp. 207–232.

characteristics. Interestingly, people neglected the base-rates even when they were provided with rather generic descriptions as well.

Information specific to a single case can sometimes appear more compelling than actual numerical odds. Often these traits are simply more obvious and we fail to moderate their influence using our background knowledge.

Relevance: You can gain a structural advantage in investing by attending to base-rates. These can offer some of the most secure opportunities, as events in business tend to be cyclical. A helpful practice is to isolate key factors in a given position and then try to identify other historical examples that can inform specific outcome likelihood. Assigning probabilities to potential outcomes is one of the best practices that we advocate for to decrease the base-rate neglect. For example, if you are considering taking a position on a software service company and you are trying to assess the probability that it may be taken over via a buyout, you can look at the history of buyouts among software service companies and determine an annual average percentage of companies taken out, the range of the number of takeovers over several years, and the average range and medium premium paid. You may then tweak your analysis based on certain factors that are unique to the company you are currently analyzing to come up with an appropriate probability of a takeout for the purpose of your analysis. Such factors could include the age of the current CEO, management's expressed willingness to consider a transaction, the level of payout for management in the event of a change of control, and the competitive position of the company. Each of these factors may have their own statistical significance with respect the probability of a takeout and can be assessed in conjunction with the initial projection to generate a reasonable assessment of the likelihood of the contingency. This process can then be repeated for each relevant factor that may have a material effect on the value of the security.

Processing Level: Base-rate neglect is an intuition bias. Like many knowledge biases, we sometimes fail to make use of relevant information because it is overridden by other compelling information that appears more salient in the moment.

Brain Mechanisms: Our brains strongly respond to colorful narratives, emotional instances, and detailed examples. By contrast, base-rate knowledge frequently lurks quietly behind the scenes outside of our conscious attention. General probabilities have a hard time standing out amid the steady stream of incoming information available. Base-rates will often remain offstage as background knowledge unless we deliberately move them front and center. The frontal lobes are key to this process.

Our reinforcement learning circuits track base-rates. We have discussed the basal ganglia as tracking probabilities in the environment, usually in reward-based learning experiments. Even in concrete and immediate examples, we can invoke probability knowledge. The challenge is knowing when to call upon these well-established responses. Since base-rates are always relevant to making accurate predictions, actively attend to them by using a process. Make it a routine to pay attention to background knowledge and especially any numerical information that you may have as you go about your work.

Who's vulnerable? Base-rate neglect is a challenge faced by many investors, since base-rates are built up over time. It can be easy to ignore information that has unfolded over the long term, but paying attention to these structural factors built into particular industries can lead to great opportunity.

Remedies:

- Rigorous quantification will help to reduce base-rate neglect. Once you have identified variables important to your position, you should seek to determine how predictable these variables are. Try to put a number to key variables through additional research on the industry and context for the position whenever possible.

- Seek to recognize the uncertainty surrounding each of your investments. This exercise emphasizes that multiple outcomes may occur. You should do the most work on researching those investments that contain high uncertainty and potentially high risk. Next, assign probabilities to various outcomes for all potential profit and loss cases. Recognizing the possibility of undesirable outcomes and quantifying their probability will often organically guide you toward considering base-rates. Seek out other historic instances and collect a sample from which to establish a base-rate probability for each factor.

- Thinking in terms of probability sets the stage for appropriate analysis of the data collected during your fundamental research. This action will again help you to identify and make use of relevant base-rates.

* also see *anchoring bias* and *salience bias* (Chapter 3)

> *Only in Britain could it be thought a defect to be too clever by half. The probability is that too many people are too stupid by three-quarters.*
>
> —John Major

II. Social Knowledge Biases

We wrap up our bias tour with a brief section on biases driven by social behavior. People can achieve remarkable results when they work together. In finance it is often helpful to track what others are thinking. These can be colleagues who have good (or poor) ideas, they can be experts on a particular industry, or they may be market participants in general. Tracking sentiment can be an important dimension of investing. If an investor has a sense of the market sentiment about the material factors affecting a business, then the investor can predict the effects of investor sentiment on prices when new information comes to light. However, it is important to make your own independent assessment and not be overly influenced by the investment narrative that has been adopted by the market, or by other investors. We can get into hot water when we are overly influenced by other people's thinking.

Knowledge Illusion

Definition: We sometimes take for granted that we understand a topic because we have heard an expert summarize it. When we trust what experts tell us, we sometimes mistakenly feel a sense that we too possess the full depth of their knowledge. In reality, we may only have a cursory understanding of the situation, as we have not engaged in the hard work of earning the knowledge ourselves. Details can be lost in translation. This phenomenon is called the *knowledge illusion*.

Background: What are your thoughts about stem cell research? In the rare case that you are an expert on the techniques, you can probably provide a highly accurate account. If you are like most people, then you may have some general opinion, but probably lack much depth on the topic. Stem cell research has been in the news periodically and was a major point of controversy during George W. Bush's presidency. Familiarity with the term and the fact that many experts know a great deal about stem cells and developmental biology can sometimes lead us to feel that we know more than we really do. Poor decisions can follow in these cases and it is hard to see them coming.

Researchers Steven Sloman and Philip Fernbach describe many instances of this cognitive error in their excellent book *The Knowledge Illusion.*[8] A particularly powerful example of the knowledge illusion was carried out by Sloman and Nathanial Rabb.[9] These researchers presented people with brief summaries of hypothetical scientific discoveries (such as the discovery of rocks that glow in the dark). Some participants in the experiment were informed that the scientific discovery team has "not yet explained" the phenomena and that they "do not yet understand" how it works. A different group of people were given the same description, but the wording was altered to indicate that the science team has "thoroughly explained" the phenomena and that they "fully understand" it. Remarkably, the participants in the experiment rated their own personal understanding of the glowing rocks as being higher in the latter case than in the former, simply because other credible individuals were described as understanding it. In other words, people in this study claimed to possess a greater understanding due to the mere mention that others understood the phenomena.

Sloman and Rabb next sought to determine whether access to the expert knowledge influenced the knowledge illusion. In this case, people were presented with a similar mysterious scientific phenomena and

---

[8]   Sloman, S., and P. Fernbach. 2018. *The Knowledge Illusion: Why We Never Think Alone.* Penguin.

[9]   Sloman, S.A., and N. Rabb. 2016. "Your Understanding is My Understanding: Evidence for a Community of Knowledge." *Psychological Science* 27, no. 11, pp. 1451–1460.

told that it was "not yet understood," "fully understood" (with knowledge freely available), or "fully understood" (but knowledge kept secret by government officials). As in the prior study, people showed a knowledge illusion by claiming to have a better understanding when reading that scientists fully understood the phenomenon, but worse understanding when scientists were described as not understanding the rocks. Interestingly, people's knowledge illusions decreased when the discovery was described as "fully understood," but that the details were not available to the public. This suggests that the knowledge illusion is most potent when others claim to understand new or complicated phenomena and that the details are available to us, yet we have not examined them for ourselves.

It is important to keep in mind that fully rational people should always claim equivalent low levels of personal knowledge about something that they do not understand. The possibility of free access to information should not be taken as evidence that we have improved our own understanding yet it often is.

Relevance: The knowledge illusion is particularly challenging when listening to expert opinion about investment opportunities. If experts confidently repeat opinions and provide cursory high-level explanations, we may begin to overestimate our understanding by outsourcing our knowledge to these other individuals. The more we listen to discussion on a stock, especially when numerous people agree on what will proceed, the more we risk falling victim to this illusion of knowledge. The knowledge illusion tends to arise in the context of interfacing with management, sell-side analysts, and other investors. We tend to adopt the confidence that is projected by those who share a compelling and articulate narrative as if we had conducted the research ourselves. It is critical that we attempt to learn the knowledge for ourselves by verifying what we are hearing others say. This is the most effective way to avoid falling into this challenging trap.

Processing Level: The knowledge illusion spans both the intuition and reason levels. This illusion emerges from a disconnect between intuition and reason. We should be focusing on carrying out deliberative analyses of a situation, but instead we fall into a mental trap by mistaking familiarity and the prospect of knowing for a factual detailed personal understanding.

Brain Mechanisms: Our brains are wired to focus on information that appears front and center. We often have difficulty gaining insight into our blind spots and this can apply toward our knowledge as well. We simply have a hard time reasoning about what is not there. Our brains just don't have the representation, so there is nothing for us to interrogate. If we do not possess a command of the facts for a given investment, it may not be readily apparent provided that the facts appear to exist and we have gained confidence from other people around us. The knowledge illusion is also created by our tendency to trust like-minded individuals. This trust can inadvertently spill over into believing we know more than we really do.

In an ironic twist on this topic, researcher Deena Skolnik Weisberg and her colleagues conducted a study on the role of neuroscience explanations in producing illusory understanding about the mind.[10] They provided brain research experts and non-experts with better and worse explanations of mental processes. In some cases, they added text about how it was known that certain brain circuitry "was involved" in the psychological processing. This superficial mention of brain involvement strengthened non-experts beliefs that they now understood the psychological function better: an illusion created by mere proximity to expert knowledge.

This study by Weisberg and her colleagues led us to put extra effort in these *Brain Mechanisms* sections to ensure that they maximally enrich your understanding of these cognitive biases. We have attempted to avoid boosting your sense of confidence merely because we have pointed out that your brain is involved in generating bias!

Who's vulnerable? Many investors may experience the knowledge illusion. Investors who tend to listen to outside opinions are likely to be particularly vulnerable. This illusion is also relevant to confirmation bias, a tendency to seek out confirmatory evidence. If you hear the same idea repeated enough times, it can begin to feel like the truth. The fact remains that the market does not care how many people claimed a particular outcome was inevitable. Anyone getting involved in a new industry is at particular risk for this bias, as they will not yet have a sound knowledge base in the area.

---

[10] Weisberg, D.S., F.C. Keil, J. Goodstein, E. Rawson, and J.R. Gray. 2008. "The Seductive Allure of Neuroscience Explanations." *Journal of Cognitive Neuroscience* 20, no. 3, pp. 470–477.

Remedies:
- Perform deep work on a topic. This will include questioning your assumptions and describing your narrative in detail to others. You should actively seek out the gaps in your own understanding of an industry, company, or competitive circumstances. If you find a gap, ask whether the degree of uncertainty requires a more cautious stance on position sizing and adjust appropriately.
- Know your "circle of competence" and appropriately weight your investment positions based on your own personal level of uncertainty. Remember that there is likely more uncertainty in the world than you think and because others are making a compelling case, this does not directly ensure that it will play out as they describe.

* also see *confirmation bias* and *groupthink biases*

> *In the media age, everybody was famous for 15 minutes. In the Wikipedia age, everybody can be an expert in five minutes. Special bonus: You can edit your own entry to make yourself seem even smarter.*
> —Stephen Colbert

Groupthink Biases

Definition: Sometimes it is wise to follow the wisdom of the crowd, or to seek a second opinion from others. Other times, group discussions can lead us astray into a situation in which we become overly confident in a poorly conceived position. The negative impacts of group decision making have been termed *groupthink*, a set of biases leading us to make suboptimal decisions because we receive too much influence from a group.[11]

Groupthink is indeed a fitting phenomenon with which to close our bias tour, as it emerges from complex group interactions and plays upon

---

[11] Janis, I.L. 1972. *Victims of Groupthink: A Psychological Study of Foreign-Policy Decisions and Fiascoes.*

many of the other biases that we have discussed in this and previous chapters.

Background: Social psychologist, Irving Janis applied the term *groupthink* to the behavior of people who are deeply involved in a cohesive in-group. Frequently the group's movement toward a unanimous viewpoint will override their ability to realistically evaluate non-favored alternatives.

Janis wrote extensively about the characteristics of groupthink and many applied instances of how its influence plays out in daily life. The conditions ripe for groupthink typically involve a small group that has worked together for a sustained period of time on a problem, or a topic. The group's shared time investment builds group cohesion and unity. After having discussed a plan, or position, the group begins to suffer from some undesirable biases.

The biases associated with groupthink are interrelated. They all emerge from group dynamics centering upon seeking agreement, then defending the agreed upon position. Some of Janis' specific groupthink biases include the following:

1. *Invulnerability* and *unanimity:* A sense of overconfidence that emerges from repeated interactions with others who bolster a commonly held position. With repetition comes an undesirable sense of confidence in the position and a singular focus on one viewpoint.
2. *Self-censorship* and *rationalization:* A group can foster self-censorship of dissenting opinions. After repeated attachment to a particular viewpoint, outside ideas, or counter-narratives can be rationalized away as being unlikely, or outright implausible.
3. *Pressure* and *"mindguarding":* Over time, a polarized group can begin to actively protect one another from hearing dissenting opinion, thereby enhancing a perceived sense of confidence and invulnerability. This can even go so far as to involve some in-group members pressuring others to avoid presenting alternative viewpoints.

Relevance: The groupthink phenomenon can be extremely insidious among investors. It can show itself among investment houses, where groups of people work on a portfolio together. It can occur within investment clubs where members share ideas. It can also occur simply by relying on the opinions of experts, or even informal colleagues.

Investment fund managers risk some of these dynamics because they are authority figures. The employees may feel a sense of loyalty, or pressure to conform to a preferred opinion, simply out of fear of not wanting to appear difficult, or "stirring the pot." This type of environment can inadvertently breed in-group thinking. Repeated discussions about a position can subtly lead to a sense that a truly correct narrative has been reached. Much like the knowledge illusion (see previous bias), the sense of unanimity and reliance on collective knowledge can bolster a weak theory and lead a group toward disaster. Over time, group members may begin to suffer from illusions of invulnerability and control that are extremely difficult to undermine once they have taken hold.

Individual investors can also suffer the effects of groupthink if they rely too much on the advice of trusted experts, or colleagues. Repeatedly hearing the same narrative offered by many people can lead to an illusion of unanimity. Once this is in place, it becomes difficult to seek out and objectively consider plausible alternative forecasts. This is a highly dangerous place to be for an investment position, as undue risk-taking may follow from this potentially toxic situation.

Processing Level: Groupthink represents a complex interaction among our instinct, intuition, and reason modes of thinking. These biases may emerge from what is initially sound reasoning that then begins to feel intuitively correct. As time moves on, the intuitive appeal of group consensus, cohesion, and a sense of invulnerability can form. Eventually, there may even be an instinctual social appeal in defending a position that several group members feel a strong sense of ownership toward.

Brain Mechanisms: Back in the 1950s, psychologist Solomon Asch provided people with an easy perception task: judge the length of a series of lines. Asch also included a group component where others were observed to collectively agree upon a wrong answer. Despite the ease of judgments, people often provided incorrect answers succumbing to social conformity and deferring to the will of the group.[12]

---

[12]   Asch, S.E. 1956. "Studies of Independence and Conformity: I. A Minority of One Against a Unanimous Majority." *Psychological Monographs: General and Applied* 70, no. 9, p. 1.

Neuroscientist, Greg Berns and his colleagues examined the brain basis of social conformity in a brain imaging study.[13] Like Asch, they presented people with a relatively simple judgment task (judging shapes) and also included feedback from other people. Accuracy was over 80 percent when people decided on their own. Their accuracy dropped to around 50 percent when they were offered incorrect input from others. When adhering to the group decision, people showed greater activity in the parietal and occipital cortex—the same areas involved in the shape judgments. When they disagreed with the group and answered correctly, they showed more activity in the basal ganglia and amygdala, areas associated with learning and emotion. In other words, the influence of other people's uniform (and wrong) ideas influenced the same brain areas actually involved in estimating the shape similarity. It is as if the bogus group input actually morphed the person's own perceptual decisions.

These findings can be extended to the groupthink biases. If people activate their judgment-related brain areas even when integrating faulty group input, this suggests that their groupthink tendencies run quite deep. It was as if the participants in the experiment could not really distinguish their own ideas from those of the group. An unsettling finding indeed.

Who's vulnerable? Investors who frequently rely upon the opinions of others are particularly vulnerable. This class of people can include fund managers, whose employees begin to form an insulated in-group. Groupthink can also affect individual investors who regularly discuss shared interests with colleagues, or rely upon the strong and coherent opinions of experts. Also at-risk are investors who dabble in positions outside of their own realm of expertise. Such individuals are open to inadequately analyzing strong sounding forecasts from people who may possess more knowledge about the area.

Remedies:

- Seek to assemble a diverse group of individuals with varied backgrounds from different disciplines. Diversity will foster consideration of diverse opinions.

---

[13] Berns, G.S., J. Chappelow, C.F. Zink, G. Pagnoni, M.E. Martin-Skurski, and J. Richards. 2005. "Neurobiological Correlates of Social Conformity and Independence During Mental Rotation." *Biological Psychiatry* 58, no. 3, pp. 245–253.

- Build a culture that welcomes dissent. Invite some dishar-mony among your group members, as we tend to drift toward consensus in groups. Try to ensure that the group members understand that a diversity of opinions is necessary for an effective decision-making process.
- Periodically refreshing the group with new members can be beneficial as well, as this will introduce new perspectives from individuals who will not share any consensus-based biases that may have formed in the existing group.
- Enhance openness about a given issue by having group mem-bers submit their concluding thoughts anonymously rather than openly.
- Designate participants to be advocates for a bull and bear on each case and then have group members reverse these roles. Also, try to talk in terms of probability and avoid the language of absolutes. This leaves the door open to multiple outcomes in any discussion.
- A group can conduct an odds-on betting pool where each participant bets based on the probability of the occurrence of certain variables that are relevant to any security that is the subject of the group's deliberations.
- Seek to quantify different aspects of a position. This will help to mitigate biases related to becoming overly certain.

* also see *confirmation bias, knowledge illusion, illusion of control* (Chapter 3), *overconfidence bias* (Chapter 3), *salience bias* (Chapter 3), *in-group bias* (Chapter 3)

> *You will do things in the name of a group that you would never do on your own. Injuring, hurting, killing, drinking are all part of it, because you've lost your identity, because you now owe your allegiance to this thing that's bigger than you are and that controls you.*
> —George Carlin

Recommended Readings

Park, W.W. 1990. "A Review of Research on Groupthink." *Journal of Behavioral Decision Making* 3, no. 4, pp. 229–245.

Sloman, S., and P. Fernbach. 2018. *The Knowledge Illusion: Why We Never Think Alone*. Penguin.

PART IV

CHAPTER 8

Best Practices to Avoid Behavioral Bias

Introduction

In the prior chapters we outlined many of the biases that haunt us and their origins within the brain. Though the specter of biases cannot be completely exorcised from our minds, we can implement procedures to mitigate their pernicious influences upon our decisions. Up to this point, we have described specific remedies related to each bias that we have covered. In this final chapter we outline some suggested best practices and procedures to enhance the decision-making process by providing safeguards and analytical speed bumps that should reduce the distortions created by biases. Some of these ideas have been mentioned in prior chapters, but here we will attempt to tie it all together with an emphasis on practical solutions.

We encourage you to take particular note of some of the strategies and tips that you believe will help you most to improve your investing process. This chapter will provide you with the most benefit if you take an active role. Feel free to develop your own outline of a personal, or team-based, investment strategy that incorporates the processes that you feel will help you the most. As you notice practices that you think would benefit you, make sure to revisit the relevant sections within the earlier chapters. This will help you make your own connections between biases and mitigation strategies. Also, be sure to check out some of our recommended readings associated with each section if they appear relevant to you.

A fool with a plan is better off than a genius without a plan!
—T. Boone Pickens

Strategy: Using a Rules-Based Investment Process

Passive Index and Quantitative Investing

The most direct method for avoiding investment bias is to remove the role of the human decision maker from the evaluation of individual investment opportunities by using a defined set of rules that are implemented automatically. This formulaic approach requires the investor to pre-determine objective criteria for favorable investment outcomes. This style of investment is quite popular today and most of the volume of the stock market is attributable to some variation of a formulaic approach. According to a 2017 study conducted by Marko Kolanovic, global head of quantitative and derivatives research at JPMorgan, about 60 percent of trading volume in stocks stems from quantitative, or passive investors.[1] This same study suggested that only 10 percent of trading volume comes from active managers.

For most investors, a consistent passive investing strategy is both a rational means to overcome the behavioral bias inherent in investment decision making and a sound practice that will typically generate results that exceed actively managing assets. A study conducted by Hendrick Bessembinder of Arizona State University evaluating the 25,782 stocks traded from 1926 to 2015 found that the top 1,000 performers (less than four percent of the total) accounted for substantially all the market's gains over the period.[2] An index will capture that top four percent, while most active managers will likely under index those super stocks. Even if an active manager is fortunate enough to have identified some of these stocks, they will often sell them along the way, as they are shaken out by the combination of behavioral bias and stock volatility. The headwinds for actively managed funds are compounded by the fact that they tend to charge fees that are three to four times those of passive index funds, which over time drastically drags on performance.

In 2017, Standard & Poor's published an annual report that found that over the last 15 years, 92 percent of actively managed large-cap

---

[1]   Kolanovic, M., and R.T. Krishnamachari. 2017. "Big data and AI strategies: Machine Learning and Alternative Data Approach to Investing." *JP Morgan Global Quantitative & Derivatives Strategy Report.*

[2]   Bessembinder, H. 2018. "Do Stocks Outperform Treasury Bills?" *Journal of Financial Economics* 129, no. 3, pp. 440–457.

funds returns lagged those of a S&P 500 index fund. Small and mid-cap actively managed funds did even worse with 93 and 95 percent of indexes respectively, outperforming their actively managed counterparts. By consistently investing in the index regardless of market conditions over a 20-year period, investors will typically outperform actively managed alternatives and can avoid the havoc caused by behavioral biases.

Another dominant form of rules-based investing is the quantitative investing approach. Rules or algorithms associated with these systems are typically structured to concentrate on factors that have historically been associated with superior market performance. These include valuation and operating (or price) momentum. Quantitative investing has become increasingly popular over the years and is typically implemented by institutional investors relying on high speed computers. One of the major challenges of a quantitative rules-based approach is that any anomaly that is exploited to generate returns in excess of the market is typically arbitraged away over time when quant investors ultimately close the gap and crowd out the opportunity. Nonetheless, these rule-based strategies that follow an investment formula are not governed by subjective human judgment and therefore avoid the associated biases.

Active managers can have a direct advantage over these strategies because human judgment is removed from the process in both quantitative and passive index-based investing. Given that both index and quantitative investing cannot discern qualitative aspects including management quality and shifting industry dynamics that require human evaluation, an opportunity exists for investors who perform quality research that focuses on these dynamics. The challenge for active managers is to evaluate these factors without succumbing to the distortions of bias.

Strategy: Active Management

Good Practices Throughout the Investment Process

Tip 1: Keep a Journal

Throughout the investment process it is helpful to keep a journal of your findings and thoughts. Keeping an investment journal is similar to a professional athlete reviewing tapes of their performance. By recording the investment process, you can reflect on your initial thoughts and assumptions made at the beginning of the process and evaluate how those views may have changed over time. It is important for you to begin the process with the understanding that the very first impressions or thoughts about an investment will likely be very different than the conclusions drawn after the research process is complete.

The process of maintaining a journal also helps to overcome memory biases including: *availability, primacy,* and *recency* biases (Chapter 5). Newly acquired information can be disproportionately emphasized, as our prior thoughts are more distant and therefore given less psychological weight. Likewise, having a running total of your work on a position will minimize the possibility that you are over-weighting early information that was used to develop the original thesis. Reviewing previous notes on more distant factors can help to mentally recalibrate their weights in relation to recent, or initial information, both of which tend to be over-represented within our minds.

Journal keeping can help you to avoid knowledge biases, notably *confirmation bias* (discussed in Chapter 7). Your initial thoughts are often substantially different than the eventual conclusions made after the investor's research process has concluded and you will be able to capture the details of these differences by maintaining a journal.

Tip 2: Record Early Viewpoints

It is often useful to write down your early assumptions before any material work is done. Many first-pass assumptions are erroneous and this will become evident as you complete more research. This exercise is important because it can help you to avoid prematurely adopting a narrative and then seeking out evidence to support it. As some of the original beliefs prove to be wrong, this should initiate a fluidity of knowledge. Analysts must continually perform self-assessments of their thinking processes—in other words, engage in meta-cognitive practices. Such self-reflection is literally thinking about one's own thinking. Regularly step back from a problem so that you can reflect upon your own thought processes. Remain openly curious about all aspects of the situation, continually reflecting upon how you are approaching the problem. Ask: "How else might I think about this from other perspectives"? "What might others be seeing that I have not yet noticed"?

You should also keep track of instances that arise in the process that could be shaded by one or more of the behavioral biases that we have discussed in the previous chapters. Make note of such instances in your investment journal so that you can examine the validity of your interpretation of the data you are reviewing. The analyst may not be the only person subject to bias. It is also helpful to take note of the possible biases held by providers of data such as management, industry, or customer contacts.

Technique: Enhancing Your Awareness of Uncertainty and Error

There are known knowns. There are things we know that we know. There are known unknowns. That is to say, there are things that we now know we don't know.

—Donald Rumsfeld

One of the most common and perilous traps that we fall into in investing is the *illusion of control* (Chapter 3), which gives us a false sense of certainty. Investors often think in terms of whether they are right or wrong with respect to a given investment thesis. This notion can often lead to judging the validity of investments and investment processes based on isolated outcomes. The world is not so discrete, rather, it is filled with uncertainty and risk. The darkness of uncertainty and risk tends to be where the shadows of behavioral biases are cast. The fortunes of any business are subject to a multitude of shifting dynamics that depend upon economic, managerial, operational, and competitive factors. We can identify, isolate, and quantify some of those factors, while others remain out of our reach to quantify. As investors and analysts, we must distinguish between the risk we can quantify and pure uncertainty, which is definitively unknown to us.

It is important to remember that our notion of the "ground truth," or of what is "real" is always merely a model of reality. We tend to overestimate the accuracy of our models of the universe when they are the state-of-the-art. People saw the world as being geocentric until Galileo provided an alternative model. That model was later refined and supplanted by the physics described by Newton's calculus, which was ultimately supplanted by Einstein's relativity. This was further refined by our knowledge of quantum mechanics. The point is that even in the physical sciences our vision of the truth in the world is not static.

The worlds of finance, business, and economics are shaped in large part by the confidence and perceptions of market participants, the disruption of developing technologies, and a myriad of macro-economic factors. The weights and probabilities associated with these factors are often difficult to discern. As a result, we must be humble and recognize that the world of investment is neither mechanical, nor definable with mathematical certainty. To think otherwise is hubris, which is the greatest sin of investors and is regularly punished by the market. Remember to keep questioning your assumptions, especially when you find yourself believing that you are full in control and know the ground truth of a situation.

Tip: Simplify, Streamline, and Focus

Given the complexity of investment analysis, it is helpful and necessary to reduce the total number of decisions that you must make. For each investment, you should focus on the most material and relevant factors. *Decision fatigue* occurs when we are faced with too many considerations (Chapter 3). With the vast amount of data that is available, it is easy to miss the forest for the trees if you leave yourself in a depleted state.

You can address this issue is by applying specific rules that lead to an automatic action item. If such a set of rules is applied with discipline, then you can reduce the items that require deliberation. Typically, sets of rules are developed over time through experience. For example, Sabrepoint Capital applies a rule that if a cyclical company generates good quarterly results and the report is followed by a decline in the share price, then it will exit the position. Through experience, the investment team at Sabrepoint Capital has learned that this circumstance is likely unwinnable in the short term, because the market will not react to good news or bad news in a positive fashion until the cycle bottoms. This rule does not require any additional deliberation and eliminates the necessity to consider next steps, thereby limiting decision fatigue and other potential biases specific to a given situation.

Rules-based practices also limit susceptibility to several biases that develop over time as we think about a position. Operating by concrete rules limits the possibility of developing an illusion of control about an investment. You can also limit exposure to the *gambler's fallacy*, *hindsight bias* (Chapter 3), and *sunk-cost effect* (Chapter 5), as these biases often develop due to sustained active thinking about an investment position.

Technique: Group Decision Making in Active Management

It is helpful to seek out multiple perspectives in order to help avoid the specific biases of any one individual. The active investment process we advocate for is based off a typical model that would be used by a professional investment team. Individual investors can duplicate this process by forming an investment club, in which different members adopt different roles for analyzing individual securities.

Bias Block: *Avoiding Groupthink Biases*

Troublesomely, working in groups can lead toward biased analysis (see Chapter 7). Groups can be pulled toward too much agreement simply by seeking harmony. We tend to unwittingly drift toward consensus when each group member is evaluated based on the merits of his thoughts and the input of others may affect how the group perceives his input. It is important that the group understands that a diversity of opinions is necessary for an effective decision-making process.

To enhance decision making it is helpful to assemble a diverse group of individuals with varied backgrounds from different disciplines. Also, the group should embrace variant viewpoints and there should be no negative consequences for dissent. Periodically refreshing the group with new members can be beneficial as well, as this will organically bring in new perspectives from individuals who will not share any consensus-based biases that may have formed. The most dangerous circumstance is when a group has built a unified consensus where each participant has adopted the bias and viewpoint of the whole. Under those circumstances, challenges to the consensus model tend to be discounted with conviction and reinforced by a diffusion of responsibility. Such are the conditions that lead to the infamous set of biases associated with *groupthink* (Chapter 7).

Additional techniques exist that can improve the effectiveness of group deliberation and decision making. One way to enhance openness about a given issue is to have group members submit their concluding thoughts anonymously rather than openly. Another possible method is to designate participants to be advocates for a bull and bear on each case and then have group members reverse these roles. Also, try to talk in terms of probability and avoid the language of absolutes. This leaves the door open to multiple outcomes in any discussion. To reinforce the effectiveness of this approach, the group can conduct an odds-on betting pool where each participant bets based on the probability of the occurrence of certain variables that are relevant to any security that is the subject of the group's deliberations. Quantifying different aspects of a position will help to mitigate biases related to becoming overly certain.

Steps in the Active Management Investment Process

To provide context to discuss the procedures that can be implemented to mitigate bias in an active investment process, we need to have a defined process to apply it to. Below is a simple diagram of a typical investment process consisting of idea generation, fundamental research, analysis, execution, and review. It is important to keep thorough records of each step in order to draw upon and refer to the data and analysis produced in the process to facilitate subsequent steps (refer to Figure 8.1).

Tip: Idea Sourcing

Most investment processes start with the generation of an investment idea. Investment ideas may originate from the identification of new macro or industry trends and speculation about the beneficiaries or victims of those changes. Ideas can also come from observing insider buying, or by following the changes in the holdings of successful investment advisors. Many investors will use fundamental investment screens based on absolute or

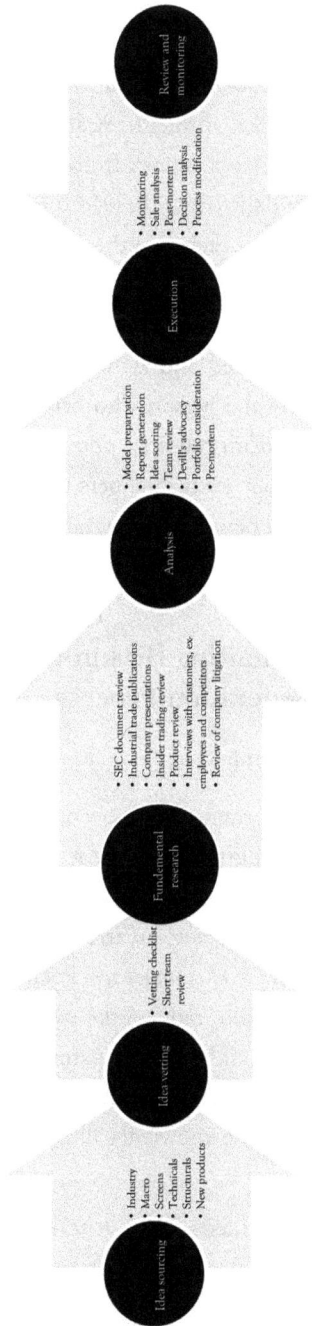

Figure 8.1 An outline of the steps involved in active investment management

relative valuation, margin improvement, sell-side analyst revisions, or return on capital. Other screens may be based on technical characteristics such as price momentum and trading volume changes, or structural factors including spin-offs, stock-based mergers, or bankruptcy emergence. Often investors will find new ideas through researching existing investments. Finally, some of the best ideas emerge from recognizing products and services that we use in our daily lives. These idea generation methods are by no means exhaustive, but in each case their generation is typically the start of the investment process. The endowment bias (Chapter 3) can become an obstacle in connection with idea sourcing. It is common that an idea is more likely to be pursued and a thesis to be less skeptically adopted when it is analyzed by the person who originated the idea. To avoid this issue, an investment team can pool potential investment ideas and they can be assigned to other team members that did not originate the ideas so that the endowment bias can be mitigated and a more critical analysis can be applied.

Strategy: Limiting Bias in the Idea Generation Process

Tip: Stick to Your Circle of Competence

When generating ideas, it is important to winnow out those that are more susceptible to bias. You can simplify things by focusing on only certain industries. This reduces the duplicative work that is necessary to ramp up the learning curve on a new industry. Warren Buffett describes this process as *staying within your circle of competence*. Focusing on industries that you are familiar with is efficient, reduces the possibly of bias-related error, and also eliminates a large number of companies that are simply not necessary to analyze. This reduced workload can also reduce the risk of decision fatigue (Chapter 3) and the knowledge illusion bias (Chapter 7).

Risks Associated with Getting Ideas from Others

It is dangerous to take investment recommendations from others whom you consider to be talented investors, or people who have had a string of successes. The *In-Group* and *Hot Hand* biases (Chapter 3) tend to be prevalent in these circumstances. With respect to the *In-Group* bias, if we adopt an investment idea that is quite popular, then we can suffer from deferring to the apparent wisdom of the crowd at the expense of our own judgment. Alternatively, if we get an investment idea from an individual investor, or analyst, who has recently enjoyed a string of successes, we may mistake a random streak of luck for genuine investment prowess. In each of these circumstances, when we then move onto the fundamental investing stage we may have a predetermined bias to seek out information that is consistent with the narrative provided by the group, or by the analyst who introduced the idea.

Bias Block: The Hot Hand and In-Group Biases

A simple remedy for overcoming the bias associated with investment ideas from others is to avoid them all together. You may want to adopt a "not made here" policy, in which you commit to the position that if you did not originate the idea then you will not pursue it. Enacting such a policy is a direct way to mitigate your risk. If you invest based on a thesis that is not widely held, then you are unlikely to face wider consequences if the thesis does not yield a successful outcome. Conversely, if you adopt a consensus view or popular narrative, when the outcome is unexpectedly disappointing everyone is likely to be headed for the exit at the same time. Investing visionary, Benjamin Graham, claimed that the quality of analysis matters most, not what the crowd is doing. Be careful about popularity and about trusting others' opinions, or you risk inheriting their biases. Since you will have no access to how they emerged, these biases will be particularly difficult to address. You will also suffer from a disadvantage relative to the prognosticator and others who are more deeply connected to the original research. When will you know that you are wrong? When would be the right time to take profits? Without doing your own work beyond the premises provided by the original proponent you will struggle to answer these questions.

Another smart idea to consider is to begin by trying to disprove an idea from someone else if you are considering borrowing their potential wisdom. Working through this process will give you more ownership of the idea and a better understanding of its fundamentals. You will end up better understanding the position through performing the evaluation. It is important to look past the advice given by a market prognosticator, or popular stock picker, and conduct your own independent evaluation of each investment thesis. If it still appears to be sound after your own investigation, then it might be appropriate for investment. If you take this route it is important to apply heightened scrutiny because of the associated risks of in-group and hot hand biases. Also, you should be mindful of the heightened risk associated with an unfavorable outcome, as it will likely lead to significantly more selling pressure than if the idea had not been widely disseminated.

Who's the more foolish, the fool, or the fool who follows him?
—Obi-Wan Kenobi

Idea Vetting

Once an idea has been sourced, an efficient practice is to vet the idea for any limitations that would preclude investment. Often times easily identified factors can rule out a particular idea. If you have hard rules that you will not violate with respect to securities that you may wish to invest in, it is prudent to make sure that the idea that you are sourcing does not violate any of those rules. For instance, if you will not invest in a company that has significant leverage, is too expensive, is too illiquid, or one in which insiders are selling stock, then it is best to check on those fundamental factors prior to conducting a more in-depth and time consuming fundamental analysis. This practice saves time and allows you to move on quickly to find the next investment prospect.

To achieve this objective, make a checklist of those factors that preclude an investment from being worthwhile and evaluate each item carefully prior to diving into a more extensive and elaborate research effort. An additional helpful step within a research team is to next prepare a short summary of the idea and discuss whether it has merit for additional consideration.

Techniques for Limiting Bias in the Idea Vetting Process

After the checklist has been applied it is often helpful to ask whether the investment candidate is subject to important factors that are too difficult to assess with any defined probability, or impact. For instance, if the investment depends heavily upon the price of an underlying commodity, such as oil, or a macro factor like the direction of interest rate policy, then it may be prudent to pass on the idea. The uncertainty surrounding those events opens the door to subjective analysis that is more susceptible to the distortions of an individual's biases.

Fundamental Research

Once an idea has been sourced and vetted, the investor will then try to glean the facts that surround it. Typically, fundamental research starts with a review of required financial disclosures, company presentations, earnings releases, and conference calls. Also, many investors will review management's stock ownership, trading patterns, and career history. Once these checks have been completed, it is common to schedule a call with management to discuss the findings. Following a discussion with management, the investor may seek other sources of information by talking to other industry participants along the value chain. These include customers, suppliers, and competitors. As a last step, review sell-side research reports and talk to other investors involved in the name in order to better understand what the market may be focused on.

Techniques for Limiting Bias in the Fundamental Research Stage

The fundamental research stage of the investment process is replete with behavioral bias pitfalls. At this stage, investors often begin to flesh out their initial premise by identifying data points that confirm or conflict with the narrative that they have adopted. During this process, *anchoring*, *confirmation bias*, and other knowledge biases (Chapter 7) tend to shade the investor's narrative development.

Bias Block: Use Inductive Reasoning to Limit Confirmation Bias

Confirmation bias may be the most powerful force that colors our reasoning when conducting fundamental research. We are all trained from an early age to use deductive reasoning. In this process, we start with a theory, review data, and then draw a conclusion. The problem with this approach is that we often solve for the theory by cherry-picking data that is consistent with our original notion and then discard or discount those facts that are inconsistent with the original theory. Fortunately you can use inductive reasoning in order to find more accurate answers. We should start with the facts absent of any general theory, then draw conclusions based on our observations. This is very difficult because we initially choose to review an investment idea based on a theory that there is opportunity determined from our initial idea sourcing process. It can be hard to step back from this initial stance.

Seek to shift the objective of your research in order to overcome the problem of solving for the answer. Instead of trying to justify the initial thesis, you can focus on completing the task for the purpose of building a collection of actionable ideas at a given price. The ultimate objective should not be to complete the research to justify investment, but rather to add the name to a collection of reviewed potential future investments. Alternatively, the analyst can start with the objective of eliminating the idea as a viable investment. This perspective change shifts the focus to the risks, as opposed to the upside. This method is more easily accomplished by separating the role of the investment team member generating the ideas from the analyst who conducts the investment research.

Assigning a designated Devil's advocate, or bear, is a third method that can reduce confirmation bias in team-based investing. It can be somewhat taxing on the resources of the team, as it requires more personnel, but it also is more likely to lead to accurate identification of the risks associated with a name compared to a process that is purely concentrated in one role.

Bias Block: Knowledge Illusion (Chapter 7)

Often in the course of researching an investment opportunity, the analyst will come upon an important technical factor that may have significant influence on the outcome of the opportunity's future prospects. In many cases, the researcher may provide too little attention to these issues, because they lack understanding and there are assumptions that are generally held or widely accepted that are then adopted by the analyst. Uncertainty is introduced when conditions change and the issue becomes material. Investors are often ill-prepared to address this uncertainty.

To overcome this risk, it first must be identified. To know if there is a possible assumption that is critical to the thesis, the analyst should seek out a disinterested party to explain it to. If there are significant gaps in the analyst's ability to explain the issue, then there is likely an important assumption being made. Take note of any such assumption and then attempt to quantify its impact. This will clarify whether the assumption is sound. Maintaining awareness of your circle of competence can help you avoid this issue. If you don't understand important factors associated with an investment candidate, then you should probably move on to seek out other opportunities.

Bias Block: Anchoring (Chapter 7)

Reviewing sell-side commentary after completing your own fundamental research offers you the opportunity to mitigate anchoring bias. If you review sell-side research early in your process, then you may be influenced by the sell-side's estimates, which could then influence your own assessment. For this reason, it is important to save any review of the sell-side, or other third-party analysis of any investment under consideration to the very end of the fundamental research process.

You should also be aware of the possibility of becoming anchored on your own conclusions once you complete your financial modeling. You should strive to avoid a static analysis that assumes only one possible outcome. Rather, you should develop multiple scenarios that factor in the outcomes of various risks and make an assessment for each case. As you monitor an investment or potential investment over time, it is important to revisit earlier assumptions and adjust them for new developments. This is similar to playing poker. When new cards are revealed, estimates of the probabilities of various outcomes should be reconsidered.

It is important to recognize that you can also use anchoring to your advantage. Investors tend to focus on minor changes to estimates of future returns despite material changes that warrant more drastic adjustment to expectations. Typically, such an adjustment will only be priced in after two-to-three new data points. If you can make an accurate assessment early on, then you can beat the crowd and adjust the investment prior to the market fully appreciating the magnitude of the shift.

Techniques for Analysis

When all fundamental research is complete, the next step in the process is to prepare a model and draft a pitch, or investment thesis report. When working with an investment team, this pitch would typically be shared with several others. An analogy can be drawn between analysis and a legal case. The fundamental research step of the investment process corresponds to the discovery portion in litigation, while the analysis stage corresponds to the trial. During the analysis phase, the idea may be scored and considered in the context of the entire portfolio for relative attractiveness and correlation with other investments. This is typically the point at which the ultimate decision to execute or forgo the idea is made. If the decision is made to execute the idea, then the sizing is determined. Finally, a road map to execute the investment is devised. It is at this time that a *pre-mortem* should be drafted. The pre-mortem and Devil's advocate portion of the analysis step are described in detail below:

Step 1: Isolate the most important factors that will determine the performance of the business

When analyzing a business and preparing the investment pitch, or report, the analyst must first isolate the constituencies involved. What is the relationship of the business to its customers, employees, vendors, and shareholders? How does the business produce its goods or services? What are the necessary inputs? How are those goods and services distributed? Who are the customers who buy those goods or services? Why do they buy those goods or services? What alternatives do the customers have? What drives the customer to buy one alternative versus another? Try to define the relationships between each of the constituencies and what variables will drive performance in the future with respect to each business.

Many of the biases we have described in the prior chapters derive from our intuition. Remember that intuitive answers may not be a true reflection of reality, even though they often feel right. Rather, they are a fit to your current mental sketch of the situation. Be vigilant about answers that feel intuitively correct. There may be other important information that you know already, or that you can dredge up with effort to accomplish higher quality analysis.

Once the material variables are isolated, you must next determine the extent to which the variables in question are predictable and quantifiable. This will help you to avoid *anchoring bias* and *base-rate neglect* (Chapter 7). For instance, in the case of an oil and gas exploration and production ("E&P") company, one obvious and powerful variable will be the price of oil. The price of oil is extremely difficult to anticipate in both the short and the long term, but will typically dictate the success or failure of any E&P company. Predicting the future price of oil requires understanding the fluctuations of both supply and demand. To understand supply, you need to understand the effects of geopolitical considerations including the stability of supply from oil producing nations, the rates of decline in the world's oil fields, the impact of new discovery, and the development and adoption of new technologies. To understand demand, you need to understand the effects of new technology and global macro cyclical conditions.

If you are investing in such positions, you should be able to determine how the rise or fall of oil prices at certain levels will impact earnings, but you are unlikely to be able to determine the probability, or magnitude of any price movements. Despite this challenge, you may be able to estimate a range of prices that are not likely to be reached in the short term. For instance, it is not likely that oil will dip below $15 or rise above $250 per barrel in the near future. This range is likely to be too broad to be useful, but it can be narrowed through additional analysis. It is important to identify the level and range of certainty surrounding each of the factors material to the business.

Recognizing the uncertainty surrounding each investment will be an important step to avoiding these biases, as it opens the door to multiple outcomes based on circumstances that are beyond the investor's ability to foresee. The greater the uncertainty and the more difficult it is to determine risk, the greater scrutiny you need to apply toward gaging your ability to anticipate risk. By isolating risk, we can work to assign probabilities to various outcomes. When discussing or thinking about various outcomes for a particular investment, it is helpful to think in terms of the probability of a desirable outcome and the magnitude of both the potential profit and loss. Recognizing the possibility of undesirable outcomes and quantifying their probability will make it much easier to recognize when an investment has gone south and that serves as a catalyst to reduce risk. This probabilistic framework sets the stage for appropriate analysis of the data collected during your fundamental research and should act to limit psychological bias associated with binary thinking.

For team-based investing, the investment team should meet during the analysis phase to review the analyst's pitch and when possible, the report of the designated bear, or Devil's advocate. Each team member should provide an assessment of the case laid out by the analysts responsible for the fundamental research. The process of evaluating the various factors that are brought up for consideration should be assessed by each team member and submitted to the ultimate decision maker.

Step 2: Develop a Simple One-Page Investment Conclusion

You should draft a simple one-page investment conclusion document at the completion of the analytical review. This document should state the premises of the assessment and a short summary of the material data that support the assessment. It should also include a roadmap for the execution of the investment and suggested actions to be taken upon various potential developments *prior to* their occurrence. This roadmap will assist the investment team in avoiding making decisions as events develop based on gut reactions in the heat of the moment. Such *in the moment* reactivity risks being colored by various memory biases discussed in Chapter 5. These include *recency, primacy*, the *endowment effect*, and the *sunk-cost fallacy*. This investment conclusion document should also include a pre-mortem analysis, which we describe next.

Step 3: Perform a Pre-mortem Analysis

The pre-mortem analysis should outline and assign probabilities to each likely scenario that could result in a positive, or negative outcome. The pre-mortem is important, as it can be referred to after the investment has been made in order to assist with execution. This may also help investors to avoid thesis drift and *confirmation bias*. The pre-mortem is also an important assessment tool once the investment has been concluded.

You can determine whether the risks have been appropriately assessed using this document. If the investment was successful, you can consider whether it adhered to the predictions and fundamental reasons set forth at the outset. By asking these questions and subsequently reviewing the pre-mortem analysis, you can identify mistakes made and biases that may have affected the investment process.

Step 4: Making the Call and Sizing the Investment

Having taken all of the preceding steps, you ultimately need to decide whether the investment is ripe. This is where the *sunk-cost effect* (Chapter 5) can be particularly dangerous. At this point, the team has expended significant time and resources evaluating the potential investment and the sheer momentum of this effort often leads to pressure to execute the investment, *even if it is not warranted*. To avoid this error, the team should use pre-set criteria for the investment. These criteria may include potential upside, potential downside, management quality, operational leverage, financial leverage, cyclicality, macro exposure, and degree of uncertainty. These criteria should be scored and the investment should be compared to the existing portfolio for correlation and risk factor exposure. The investment should be included in the portfolio based on the roadmap outlined in the investment conclusion summary document if the investment score proves to be attractive relative to alternatives. The investment should also be sized correctly as a risk mitigation tool based on the degree of uncertainty and risk of loss upon an unfavorable outcome.

Step 5: Execution

After a decision to invest has been made in the analysis stage, the idea should be executed in a manner consistent with the road map. Perhaps the most dangerous bias that can arise during the execution phase is the *curse of knowledge* (Chapter 7). After having performed extensive research on a given investment prospect, it is important that you proceed to execute in accordance with the investment roadmap. Note that the price of the investment will invariably fluctuate. Ominously, this fluctuation can serve as a sort of Rorschach test for an investment manager. As he sees price fluctuation, he may begin to assume that others see what he sees, or that other investors are recognizing negative developments as the predicted bearish scenario develops.

One means to overcome this challenge is to simply hand the investment to your trader or broker with instructions on how to execute. At this point, you do not need to make any further alterations unless you have incremental material information that significantly shifts the probabilities of a favorable or unfavorable outcome. In the event of a new development, you should review the investment conclusion and pre-mortem to avoid *primacy bias, recency bias* (Chapter 5), or *salience bias* (Chapter 3).

Step 6: Review and Monitoring

After an investment idea is executed, subsequent monitoring is usually conducted to determine if there needs to be some adjustment to the plan of execution. If any material development occurs that may require a change in the plan of execution, it is typically worthwhile to review the initial investment thesis prior to making any significant changes. It is prudent to then conduct a post-mortem once the investment is concluded.

Step 7: Perform a Post-Mortem

At the conclusion of every investment, the investment team should conduct a post-mortem. The post-mortem should be evaluated with the investment conclusion summary and the pre-mortem to determine if the original analysis adequately anticipated the ultimate result and if the probabilities assigned to each potential outcome seem reasonable in retrospect. The post-mortem is an essential mechanism to refine the investment process. One potential bias that comes into play during the post-mortem review is *hindsight bias* (Chapter 3). Often, bad *outcomes* are confused with bad *process*. However, in many cases the process was not flawed, but the outcome was dictated by identified risks that ultimately came to fruition. With very few exceptions there are always risks that are the subject of probabilistic outcomes that can unfold resulting in undesirable outcomes. In order to learn from the post-mortem process, it is important to work to distinguish unfortunate outcomes from genuine process mistakes. One very telling sign of a mistake is if the outcome, whether favorable or unfavorable, was totally unforeseen in the process. You can improve your craft and skill as an investor by engaging in this practice. If there is a lesson to be learned in any given post-mortem, the lesson should be recorded, and the investment process should be appropriately adjusted.

Bias Block: Overcoming the Default Effect, Endowment Effect, and Sunk Cost Fallacy

After an investment is made and circumstances change, whether it is a change in the factual circumstances surrounding the fundamentals of an investment, or simply a change in the security price, managers tend to be reluctant to act. This can be exacerbated by the *default effect* (Chapter 3), in which we tend to stick with something we are already engaged in. In the case of a security that has worked, the manager may tend to over-emphasize the bullish narrative associated with the idea and focus on undesirably conforming to evidence as it develops. There are a number of remedies to overcome this effect.

One effective remedy against this default effect, or status quo bias, is to ask *whether you would have the position on today at it's current size if you did not already own it.* In many cases, you would come to the conclusion that you would not buy it at the current price, or that the position would be much smaller. In these instances, it is wise to reduce the position to the appropriate size or take profits based on the outcome of this inquiry. You may conduct a similar exercise with respect to the entire portfolio where you reconstruct the portfolio at the appropriate size for each position given the current circumstances. If there is significant variance between the idea and the current configuration, then you should probably adjust the current configuration to meet the appropriate size.

During the review process, it is helpful to refer to the earlier pre-mortem that had been drafted during the initial stages of your process. You should ask yourself "what has changed since you performed your initial assessment?." If the position is close to, or has surpassed your initial target, or if the catalysts that you had identified have been exhausted, then you should be inclined to reduce, or close the position. Taking action to reduce or close certain well-performing positions tends to be most appropriate for value names that possess limited, if any, competitive advantage or growth. If the prospects for improvement in the business do not continue, then the upside is limited.

With respect to positions that have not resulted in a successful outcome, a stop-loss level can be effective as a means to overcome *default* (Chapter 3), *endowment,* or *sunk cost* effects (Chapter 5). We often feel that we have committed so much work to a project, or that the pain of a loss is too much to bear, that we hesitate to take a position off as events play out if the price moves against us. Limiting your losses is part of being a successful investor. The stop-loss should be determinative unless you have a near-term catalyst that has yet to be realized and is truly unappreciated by the market. Remember that hope is not a strategy! If the price continues to decline making the position a greater value, then you can always revisit it later. This often proves difficult for investors, as the loss is painful and associated with the security that you sold to control risk. To overcome this displeasure you may wish to force yourself to revisit the name after sufficient time has passed to avoid a wash sale.

Bias Block: Consistency and Expectancy Bias Remedies

Often we have an idea that we really like and we have advocated for it's merits in the presence of others. In some cases, other investors may invest in your idea. This situation can create a burden on you, as it may encourage you to want to avoid appearing inconsistent if you change your ideas on the position (see *consistency bias,* Chapter 5). We can also start to see what we expect to see in incoming information if we have over-committed to a position (see *expectancy bias,* Chapter 5). There are a few suggested practices to overcome these tendencies. First, you may consider avoiding any advocacy for a particular investment idea you favor outside of your investment group, or team. With those that you do share the idea with, you should emphasize the risks and provide them with a probabilistic assessment of success. You may want to acknowledge that it is a desirable bet, but that it may not a desirable outcome if the risks come to fruition. You may also mention that your opinion could change as things develop. Having voiced alternative and unfavorable outcomes, you will not appear inconsistent if you change your mind. You will also guard against becoming over-committed and seeing what you expect to see according to your favored narrative. Sometimes it helps to say that this is your opinion based on the facts that you see them, but also remind others that your opinion could change at any time if you acquire other information, or if the hand of fate tips to favor the risks in your assessment.

Technique: Make a Playbook to Constantly Improve Your Process

One of the reasons it is wise to keep an investment journal is that it helps you record the process for each investment so that you can evaluate outcomes and learn from them. We suggest that you maintain a separate journal that serves as your playbook. This journal summarizes the lessons you have learned in your journey to becoming an ever more successful investor. You should treat the playbook as a *living document*, one that will be constantly amended as new lessons are learned. We suggest that the playbook should outline your process and have a guide for investing in certain industries and under certain conditions. Ultimately the playbook can be a powerful tool for learning, honing, and refining your investment process.

Parting Thoughts

We appreciate you taking the time to read this book. Over the past eight chapters we have served as your guides on the mission of understanding behavioral biases. We've discussed a total of 25 common biases organized around how the cognitive architecture of our minds lead us into these thought traps. We've also offered you a variety of strategies, tips, and specific methods that you can use to guard against these biases eroding your financial performance. As we wrap up, we'd like to leave you with a few final take home messages.

To best use this book, we advise that you consider your own tendencies. This may require some self-reflection. Engage your brain's default mode network and genuinely reflect on your cognitive style, your investing style, and your personality. There may be some biases that you see in yourself. Others may appear to be specters that could potentially appear in your work. Still others you may already block effectively with your own methods. Not everyone is equally haunted by each of these biases, but most of us will fall prey to their influence at some point. A bias check may also include speaking to colleagues about their observations of your tendencies and style. They may detect blind spots in your methods that you cannot see. You can return the favor and both of you may emerge as stronger performers.

After completing an evaluation, we recommend that you make active adjustments to your daily work. Adjust your process and focus on evaluating a set of specific markers for success. These may include matching your pre-mortem analysis to your post-mortem analysis and scoring the consistencies and inconsistencies. Simply revisiting your journal entries on a position and noting how closely you stuck to your original thesis can help you to better understand the biases that you are most susceptible to. Focus on refining your processes and stronger outcomes will follow.

Becoming a better investor is a never-ending endeavor. We hope that this book has provided you with some insight into not only your own biases, but those of other market participants. Part of the challenge is to recognize how your thinking is influenced by bias and to adjust your process to compensate. The next step is to consider how other market participants may be influenced by their own biases and are inappropriately pricing securities as a result. Those instances create an opportunity for you to profit from the fallacies of human decision making. To aid you in your pursuit to master the flaws in human decision making, we encourage you to take an active role in shaping your work through your use of this book. Mark it up, make notes in the margins, place check marks next to sections that you plan to revisit. Knowledge about bias is only the first step. It is through rigorous self-examination and market observation that you can truly refine your process to lever the distortion of human bias on your path to becoming an exceptional investor.

If you know the enemy and know yourself, you need not fear the result of a hundred battles. If you know yourself but not the enemy, for every victory gained you will also suffer a defeat. If you know neither the enemy nor yourself, you will succumb in every battle.

-Sun Tzu, *The Art of War*

About the Authors

Daniel C Krawczyk is Professor of Behavioral and Brain Sciences and holds the Francis Chair in Brain Health at The University of Texas at Dallas. He is also a faculty member in the Department of Psychiatry at the University of Texas Southwestern Medical Center. He authored the book *Reasoning: The Neuroscience of How We Think* in 2017, a comprehensive guide to research on human reasoning. His research has focused on understanding reasoning and decision making through a multi-disciplinary approach that combines brain imaging, cognitive psychology, and studies of individuals who have sustained brain injuries. He has investigated the brain basis of reasoning in healthy people and individuals with disorders including dementia, brain injury, and autism spectrum disorders. He has led multiple Department of Defense-funded research studies evaluating people's improvements in thinking and cognitive performance. He holds a Ph.D. from the University of California, Los Angeles and was a Ruth L. Kirschstein Fellow at the University of California, Berkeley.

George H Baxter has been a professional strategic gamer, practicing corporate lawyer and hedge fund portfolio manager. He is currently the CEO and Portfolio manager at Sabrepoint Capital Management, a long/short hedge fund based in Dallas. George was previously a partner with Hirzel Capital Management, a long/short equity hedge fund based in Dallas. Prior to becoming an investment professional, George was a private equity attorney with Weil, Gotshal and Manges. George is a CFA charter holder. He graduated from University of Texas School of Law and holds a BA from Texas A&M University. Prior to attending law school, George was a professional strategic game player and author. George has a passion for strategic thought and has authored nine books and numerous articles on the topic.

Dan and George co-host the Mental Models Podcast covering topics related to the brain and finance. Please visit www.mentalmodels.com for more information.

Index

Abramson, Lyn, 53
Action potential, 5
Active management
  groupthink in, 157–158
  investment process, 158–160
  strategies, 153–155
  techniques, 155–160
Affect bias, 101–104
  background, 101–103
  brain mechanisms, 103–104
  definition, 101
  processing level, 103
  relevance, 103
  remedies, 104
  risks of, 104
Allegory of the Cave
    (Plato), xiv
Alloy, Lauren, 53
Amazon, 48
Anchoring bias, 127–131, 165
  background, 127–129
  brain mechanisms, 129–130
  definition, 127
  processing level, 129
  remedies, 130–131
  risks of, 130
Apple, 48
Arkes, Hal, 99
Asch, Solomon, 144
Atkinson, Richard, 69
Atkinson-Shiffrin model
    of memory, 69
Attention biases, 8
  focused, 29–30
Autobiographical memories,
    66–67
Availability bias, 86–88
  background, 86
  brain mechanisms, 87
  definition, 86
  processing level, 87
  relevance, 86–87

  remedies, 88
  risks of, 87
Axons, 5

Bad Religion (band), 67
Baddeley, Alan, 78
Bartlett, Frederick, 114–115
Base-rate neglect, 135–138
  background, 135–136
  brain mechanisms, 136–137
  definition, 135
  processing level, 136
  relevance, 136
  remedies, 137–138
  risks of, 137
Baumeister, Roy, 58
Baxter,George, 125
Beatty, Jackson, 23
Bechara, Antoine, 102
Behavioral bias, 3–4
  categorizing biases, 7–10
  challenges of, xx–xxii
  one-page investment conclusion
    document, 168
  parting thoughts, 173–174
  practices to avoid, 151–174
  pre-mortem analysis, 168–169
  sizing investment, 169
  strategies, active management,
    152–155
  techniques for analysis, 166–173
Behavioral finance, xv–xvi
Berger, Theodore, 112
Berns, Greg, 145
Bessembinder, Hendrick, 152
Bhatt, Meghana, 126
Bias(es)
  affect, 101–104
  anchoring, 127–131
  attention, 8
  availability, 86–88
  behavioral. See Behavioural bias

confirmation, 131–35
consistency, 95–98
emerging from our brain, 2
expectancy, 104–107
framing, 20, 41–44
groupthink, 120, 142–146
hindsight, 44–47
hot hand, 50–52
in-group, 47–49
knowledge, 9–10
memory, 8–9
overview, 1–2
optimism, 36–39
preview of memory, 81–82
recency, 75, 91–93
salience, 30–33
social knowledge, 138
Biased memory, 71
Blumer, Catherine, 99
Brain
  attention and, 15–27
  behavioral bias, 3–4
  biases from, 2
  learning system in, 113–114
  memory and, 65–66
  overview, 4–7
  as pattern matching system,
    111–113
  structuring knowledge in, 114–115
  See also Knowledge; Memory
Brain networks, 15

Camerer, Colin, 124, 126
Catastrophic errors, 54
Chapman, Gretchen, 33
Cognitive dissonance, 96
Cognitive illusions related to
    attention, 52
Collins, Rebecca, 30
Confirmation bias, 131–35
  background, 131–132
  brain mechanisms, 132–133
  definition, 131
  processing level, 132
  relevance, 132
  remedies, 133–134
  risks of, 133

using inductive reasoning to limit,
    163–164
Consistency bias, 95–98
  background, 96–97
  brain mechanisms, 97
  definition, 95–96
  processing level, 97
  relevance, 97
  remedies, 97–98
  risks of, 97
Consolidation process, 75
Cooper, Joel, 96
Cordaro, Lucien, 105
Curley, Shawn, 89
Curse of knowledge, 124–127, 169
  background, 124–125
  brain mechanisms, 126
  definition, 124
  processing level, 125
  relevance, 125
  remedies, 127
  risks of, 126

Decision fatigue, 57–61
  background, 57–59
  brain mechanisms, 59–60
  definition, 57
  processing level, 59
  relevance, 59
  remedies, 60–61
  risks of, 60
Deep processing, 76–77
Default effect, 33–36
  background, 33–34
  brain mechanisms, 34–35
  definition, 33
  overcoming, 171–172
  processing level, 34
  relevance, 34
  remedies, 35–36
  risks of, 35
Default mode network, 18, 20
Deliberative mode, 15
Descriptive model, xiii
Disposition effect, 42
Distorted memories, 79–81, 82
Distorted perception, 119–120
Doll, Bradley, 133

Dopamine, 18

Embodied cognition, 116
Emotion, 76
Endowment effect, 93–95
    background, 93–94
    brain mechanisms, 94–95
    definition, 93
    overcoming, 171–172
    processing level, 94
    relevance, 94
    remedies, 95
    risks of, 95
Equifax, 30–31
Expectancy bias, 104–107
    background, 104–105
    brain mechanisms, 106
    definition, 104
    processing level, 106
    relevance, 105–106
    remedies, 106–107
    risks of, 106
External thinking, 20

FAANG, 48
Fast/intuitive thinking, 15
Fernbach, Philip, 139
Festinger, Leon, 96
Fischhoff, Baruch, 44
Focused attention biases, 29–30
Framing bias, 20, 41–44
    background, 42
    brain mechanisms, 43
    definition, 41–42
    processing level, 43
    relevance, 42–43
    remedies, 44
    risks of, 43–44
Framing effects, 42
Fundamental research, 163–165
Fuster, Joaquin, 6, 67

Gailliot, Matthew, 58
Gambler's fallacy, 55–57
    background, 55–56
    brain mechanisms, 56–57
    definition, 55
    processing level, 56

relevance, 56
remedies, 57
risks of, 57
Gilbert, Daniel, 58
Google, 48
Graffin, Greg, 67
Grafman, Jordan, 114
Graham, Benjamin, 49, 161, xvi–xvii
Grey matter, 5
Groupthink biases, 120, 142–146
    avoiding, 157–158
    background, 143
    brain mechanisms, 144–145
    definition, 142–143
    invulnerability and unanimity, 143
    pressure and mindguarding, 143
    processing level, 144
    relevance, 143–144
    remedies, 145–146
    risks of, 145
    self-censorship and rationalization,
        143
Gurewitz, Brett, 67

Hemispheres, 6
Heuristic, overview, 1–2
Hindsight bias, 44–47
    background, 44–45
    brain mechanisms, 46
    definition, 44
    processing level, 46
    relevance, 45–46
    remedies, 46–47
Hot hand effect, 50–52
    background, 50
    brain mechanisms, 51
    definition, 50
    idea generation process in,
        161–162
    relevance, 50–51
    remedies, 51–52
    risks of, 51
Human judgement, role of, xx
Human subjectivity, xv

Idea generation process
    limiting bias in, 160–162
    risks associated with, 160–162

Idea sourcing, 158–160
Idea vetting, 162–163
Illusion of control, 52–55
  background, 53
  brain mechanisms, 54
  definition, 52
  processing level, 54
  relevance, 53–54
  remedies, 54–55
  risks of, 54
Individual knowledge biases, 123–124
Information complexity, 16
In-group bias, 47–49
  background, 47
  brain mechanisms, 48–49
  definition, 47
  idea generation process in,
      161–162
  processing level, 48
  relevance, 47–48
  remedies, 49
  risks of, 49
Instinct level, 17–18
The Intelligent Investor (Graham),
    xvii
Internal thinking, 20–21
Intuition level, 18–20
Intuitive mode, 15
  level of, 16
Investing, brain network view of,
    24–26
Invulnerability, 143
Irrational decision makers, xiii–xv
Ison, James, 105

Janis, Irving, 143

Kahneman, Daniel, 23, 42, 86, 94,
    135
Karlsson, Niklas, 39
Kliger, Doron, 86
Knetsch, Jack, 93
Knowledge
  acquiring and updating, 111
  bias. see Knowledge bias
  curse of, 124–127, 169
  distorted perception, 119–120
  filtering work, 116–117

priming and, 117–118
questions and, 118–119
See also Brain; Memory
Knowledge bias, 9–10
  individual, 123–124
  preview of, 120
  social, 138
Knowledge illusion, 138–142,
    164–165
  background, 139–140
  brain mechanisms, 141
  definition, 138
  fundamental research on, 164–165
  processing level, 140
  relevance, 140
  remedies, 142
  risks of, 141
The Knowledge Illusion (Sloman and
    Fernbach), 139
Kolanovic, Marko, 152
Krawczyk, Daniel, 57
Kressel, Laura, 33
Kudryavtsev, Andrey, 86

Learning system in brain, 113–114
Levin, Irwin, 42
Limiting bias
  in fundamental research, 163
  in idea generation process,
      160–162
  in idea vetting, 162–163
Lobes, 6
Locus coerulous-norepinephrine (LC-
    NE) activity, 22–24
Loewenstein, George, 124
Long-term memory, 71
Lynch, Peter, 43

Madrian, Brigitte, 33
McNaughton, Bruce, 79
Memory bias, 8–9, 85–86
Memory(ies)
  altered states in, 67–69
  Atkinson-Shiffrin model of, 69
  biased, 71
  biases, preview of, 81–82
  and brain, 65–66
  deep processing, 76–77

distortions and, 65–66
distortions of, 79–81
emotion, 76
formation, 72–74
long-term, 71
multiple memory systems, 69–72
personal, 66–67
retrieval, 77–79
sensory, 70
short-term, 70
strength, 72
visualization of, 74–75
working, 70–71
See also Brain; Knowledge
Mental blind spot, 3–4
Mental model, 7
Metacognition, 82
Mindguarding, 143
Mitchell, Jason, 129
Modern investing, complexities of, xvii–xx
Multiple memory systems, 69–72

Net present value (NPV), xiv
Netflix, 48
Neurons, 5
Norepinephrine, 22
Normative model, xiii

O'Keefe, John, 72
Optimism bias, 36–39
    background, 36–37
    brain mechanisms, 38
    definition, 36
    processing level, 38
    relevance, 37–38
    remedies, 38–39
    risks of, 38
Ostrich effect, 39–41
    background, 39
    brain mechanisms, 40–41
    definition, 39
    processing level, 40
    relevance, 39–40
    remedies, 41
    risks of, 41

Passive index, 152–153
Pattern matching system, brain as, 111–113
Perception-action cycle, 6, 67–68
Personal memories, 66–67
Perspective taking, 126
Pre-mortem analysis, 168–169
Pressure and mindguarding, 143
Primacy effect, 88–91
    background, 88–90
    brain mechanisms, 90
    definition, 88
    processing level, 90
    relevance, 90
    remedies, 90–91
    risks of, 90
Priming, 117–118
Psychological priming, 118

Quantitative investing, 152–153
Questions, and knowledge, 118–119

Rationalization, 143
Reason level, 20–24
Recency bias, 75, 91–93
    background, 91
    brain mechanisms, 92
    definition, 91
    processing level, 92
    relevance, 91
    remedies, 92–93
    risks of, 92
Reflected condition, 126
Response time, 16
Retrieve memory, 77–79
    cues to, 77–78
    sleep, 78–79
Risk framing, 42

Salience bias, 30–33
    background, 30
    brain mechanisms, 31–32
    definition, 30
    processing level, 31
    relevance, 30–31
    remedies, 32–33
    risks of, 32

Schemas, 114
Schultz, Wolfram, 18
Securities analysis, nature
      of, xvi–xvii
Self-assessments, 154
Self-censorship, 143
Self-reflection, 154
Sensory memory, 70
Shea, Dennis, 33
Shiffrin, Richard, 69
Short-term memory, 70
Sleep, 78–79
Sloman, Steven, 139
Slow/analytical thinking, 15
Social knowledge biases, 138
Spikes, 5
Stratton, George, 119
Structured-event complexes, 114
Structuring knowledge in brain,
      114–115
Sunk cost effect, 98–101
   background, 98–99
   brain mechanisms, 99–100
   definition, 98
   overcoming, 171–172
   processing level, 99
   relevance, 99

remedies, 100–101
risks of, 100

Tamir, Diana, 129
Task network, 21
Thaler, Richard, 94
Tracts, 5
Tversky, Amos, 42, 86, 135

Unanimity, 143

Van Bevel, Jay, 48
Visualization, 74–75

The War of the Ghosts (Bartlett),
      114–115
Wason, Peter, 131
Weber, Martin, 124
Weinstein, Neil, 36
Weisberg, Deena Skolnik, 141
White matter, 5
Work knowledge, filtering, 116–117
Working memory, 70–71

Yates, Frank, 89

Zanna, Mark, 96

www.ingramcontent.com/pod-product-compliance
Lightning Source LLC
Chambersburg PA
CBHW061218220326
41599CB00025B/4685